Praise from Industry Experts

"**If you are in the market for a new horse trailer, this is a must-read.** Brad does an excellent job of explaining all the differences in trailer design, construction, and layout. I have been buying trailers for 40 years and I learned that I really didn't know what I was doing, especially when it comes to aluminum trailers. Don't buy your next trailer till you read this."

GLENN HEBERT

Founder of the Horse Radio Network and Host of
Horses in the Morning, one of the longest-running
daily podcasts with over 3,200 episodes. He is also the
Director of Podcasting at Equine Network, leading the
largest podcast network for horse lovers worldwide.

"**This isn't just a technical manual; it's a labor of love, written by someone who has dedicated years to understanding how horses travel safely and what it takes to create or maintain a trailer that meets those needs.** This guide is a true testament to Brad's expertise and commitment to the well-being of horses on the road. Right away it's evident that he understands the intricacies of horse trailers—how they are designed, how they function, and most importantly, how they must be maintained to ensure the safety of both the horse and the driver. The depth of knowledge shared is impressive, with detailed insights! What really stands out, though, is Brad's clear love for the subject."

MICHAEL & KELSEY GASCON

Michael is the #1 Gaited Horse Trainer in the World with
over 50 National Championships. Kelsey is a Professional
Trick Rider and 2016 North American Trick Riding
Champion. They are co-owners and co-CEOs of Gascon
Horsemanship, a globally recognized equine training facility.

The Honest-to-Goodness Truth About HORSE TRAILERS

A COMPREHENSIVE GUIDE TO SAFETY, MAINTENANCE, AND PURCHASING

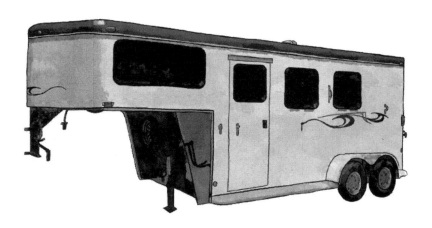

By Brad Heath

ISBN print 979-8-218-60666-4

ISBN e-book 979-8-218-61062-3

Copyright © 2025 by Brad Heath

Book design, editing, and production by Krafted, LLC | kraftedonline.com

All rights reserved.

No portion of this book may be reproduced in any form without written permission from the publisher or author, except as permitted by U.S. copyright law.

Contents

Foreword   VIII

Introduction by Brad Heath   X
    My Farming Roots
    The Importance of Choosing the Right Horse Trailer
    Overview of This Writing

1. The Anatomy of a Horse Trailer   1
    Horse Trailer Construction: Materials and Methods

2. Understanding Trailer Configurations & Their Purposes   28
    Basic Configurations
    Specialized Configurations

3. Design Elements & Horse Trailer Features   50
    Let's Break Down Some Key Trailer Features
    Exploring Different Types of Roofs, Floors, Walls, and Insulation
    Walls and Insulation
    The Importance of Ventilation and Lighting in Trailer Design

4. Trailer Mechanics & Hardware 72
   Tires and Suspension Systems: Choices and Maintenance
   Door Latches, Hinges, and Other Hardware: Functionality and Durability
   Understanding Warranties and What They Cover

5. Towing Safety & Vehicle Compatibility 99
   What is weight distribution?

6. Safety First 109
   Essential Safety Features in Horse Trailers
   Essential First Aid Supplies
   Essential Resources and Contacts

7. Horse Comfort & Welfare 117
   Loading and Unloading Techniques to Minimize Stress and Risk of Injury
   Trailer Modifications for Easier Loading and Unloading

8. Trailer Maintenance & Upkeep 124
   Regular Maintenance Checks
   Cleaning Your Trailer
   Storing and Securing Your Trailer

9. Legal & Compliance 133
   Key Federal Requirements for Horse Trailer Owners

10. Buying Guide 138
    Getting Started
    The Right Horse Trailer Makes ALL the Difference

Recap of Key Points	149
Final Thoughts from Brad Heath	151
About the Author	153
Glossary of Terms	155
Frequently Asked Questions	160
Chapter	165

Foreword

Brad Heath's *The Honest-to-Goodness Truth About Horse Trailers* is a must-read for any horse owner who hauls. Trust me, I've learned that firsthand. Having been around horses my whole life—trail riding as a kid, barrel racing, and now owning racehorses for the past 25 years—I've hauled horses all over. With seven racehorses constantly on the road, I know how crucial a good trailer is.

These horses are athletes; they need to arrive relaxed and ready to perform. That all starts with a comfortable, well-ventilated trailer, and it makes a huge difference. If you've ever struggled with trailer choices or worried about your horse's comfort, this book has the answers.

Brad is a real horseman and a hard worker. (He interviewed me for his podcast, and I could tell his passion for horse safety and comfort runs deep!) He cuts through the jargon and delivers straightforward advice and real-world tips. Whether you're hauling your first horse or managing a competitive stable like mine, you'll appreciate his focus on safety, comfort, and practical solutions.

Brad dives into the questions that matter: How do you choose the right materials? What's the best way to ensure proper ventilation? How do you avoid common safety problems? With decades of experience, he shares his expertise in an approachable way, blending technical advice with great stories that make it an enjoyable read.

So grab a coffee, settle in, and get ready to learn from one of the best. You'll gain the confidence to choose the perfect trailer and the peace of mind knowing your horses are traveling safely. This isn't just a manual; it's a must-have for every horse owner who hauls.

MILES HENRY

Miles Henry is the founder of HorseRacingSense.com and author of The Equine Business Bible and Horse Sense. As a licensed racehorse owner and member of the AQHA and The Jockey Club, he has extensive experience in both Thoroughbred and Quarter Horse racing, barrel racing, and quality horse care.

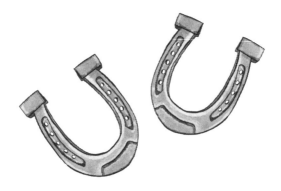

Introduction by Brad Heath

Hello, and welcome, fellow horse enthusiasts. My name is Brad Heath, and I have spent over half my life (almost 30 years now) immersed in the world of horse trailers. Ever since I was a young boy, growing up on a farm and riding horses, I have had a deep passion for not only the trailers themselves but also for the safety and comfort they provide to both horses and their owners.

Over the years, I've encountered thousands of questions, misconceptions, and challenges surrounding horse trailers. After witnessing countless horse owners struggle with confusing terminology, safety concerns, and unexpected trailer woes — not to mention mixed advice and often deceptive sales tactics used by many trailer manufacturers and dealers — it became clear to me that a comprehensive guide was needed. This guide would serve as a trusted friend and advisor to those navigating this important aspect of horse ownership.

I've poured almost 30 years of knowledge and my personal experience into this book. There's a wide range of topics — from the intricacies of choosing the right trailer, to the nuances of maintenance and safety, this guide covers it all. I want to share with you not only the technical details but also the insights that come from years of experience in the field.

There will be no "fluff" here, only commonsense answers from an honest southern country boy.

I've been riding horses as long as I can remember. Here, my dad (left) is sitting astride my Standardbred horse, named Brandy. I am on the right on my uncle's quarter horse, named Chief.

I've seen firsthand how the right trailer can make all the difference in a horse's travel experience, and I've also witnessed the dangerous consequences of poor choices and lack of knowledge in this area. Choosing the right horse trailer is more than just a purchase; it's a commitment to your horse's safety and comfort.

To bring these points home, I'll share with you a few stories from my journey — from hauling horses in cattle trailers when I was a kid, to selling trailers as a young adult, and ultimately designing and building trailers with the goal of making the industry safer. These experiences have shaped my understanding and approach to horse trailers, and I hope they will offer you both guidance and assurance.

The goal of this book is simple: to empower you with the knowledge and confidence to make informed decisions about horse trailers. Whether you're a first-time buyer or a seasoned owner, there's something in here for you.

As you turn these pages, I encourage you to embrace the journey of learning and discovery. Owning a horse trailer is a significant part of the equestrian lifestyle, and it should be approached with the same care and dedication you give to your horses.

Thank you for joining me on this journey. Together, let's explore the world of horse trailers and give our equine companions a safe, comfortable, and enjoyable experience.

Happy trailering,

Brad Heath

My Farming Roots

Tobacco, corn, and beans. That's what my dad and his two brothers grew up farming. My childhood and teenage years were spent working on the family farm. It was a lot of manual labor and taught me the value of hard work — really hard work! There's nothing quite like getting your hands dirty working the earth below your feet. It was a simple but satisfying life we lived together in Pink Hill, North Carolina.

Then came the early '80s, when seemingly overnight, the farming industry did a 180. Droughts, skyrocketing interest rates, and plummeting land values forced thousands of farmers into bankruptcy. Dad knew he either needed to add on more acreage and grow the farm business, or get out altogether. So in 1983 my dad and his brothers (and my grandfather, who I called PA) liquidated their farming equipment and invested in turkey farming.

On my dad's farm alone we had 30,000 turkeys, which required work seven days per week. Church was a big part of our lives growing up (and is today). Sunday mornings I would wake up at the crack of dawn to fire up the golf cart and make my way down to the turkey houses. We finished work by 9 AM so we could be at church by 9:45 AM. It was a wonderful life for my dad, my mom, me, and my siblings. We had a lot of fun working together and made a decent living raising turkeys for Carroll's Foods.

Fast forward to 1992. It was my senior year in high school. I was sitting at the end of the turkey house in my dad's old truck with my Uncle Doug. Dad said he had an idea: "grass sprigging." Dad was a visionary and had a knack for good business ideas. They named the business "Double D Grass Sprigging" — one D for Uncle Douglas, and one for my dad, Donald. My dad and uncle initially had a hog farm together which was named Double D Farms. So, Double D Grass Sprigging, and eventually Double D Trailers, seemed like a no-brainer.

We spent those years growing Bermuda grass — a fast-growing, drought-resistant, vibrantly colored grass. If you own a horse farm or pasture in eastern North Carolina, your horses probably graze on Bermuda grass. The first year of our grass sprigging business with Dad and Uncle Doug, we planted over 1,200 acres of Bermuda grass, and the second year we planted over 2,000 acres. We mostly planted on hog farms, since that's such a huge industry in Pink Hill, NC.

That led us into the electric fencing business. Each hog farm that had Bermuda grass needed cattle to eat it, and a fence to keep the cattle from wandering off. And the cattle needed taking care of.

From there, we added cattle equipment, and in 1994 we opened a retail store for farm equipment and animal health products. We had everything from horse feed and horse tack to vaccines, wormers, tractors, and hay balers. It was pretty much like today's Tractor Supply Co., except with even more products and services.

Now, in Eastern North Carolina, there are a LOT of horses — mostly for western pleasure and trail riding. Then, of course, there are a lot of cattle. To start, we stocked our store with all sorts of feed and animal health supplies: dewormers, medicine, horse feed, dog food, cattle feed, rabbit supplies ... you name it, we had it!

Over time, we continued to add larger-ticket products like cattle equipment, hay balers, commercial grass mowers, and yes, even horse trailers. Those first trailers were basic open stock trailers which farmers could use to haul their cows and/or horses. Gradually, the demand for more horse specific trailers began to rise as people looked for fancier saddle compartments, partitioned layouts, and better safety features.

I had always had horses and loved riding. I even remember one year we sponsored the "Double D Trail Ride," where we proudly hosted more than 300 horses and their riders. I got to lead the ride and it was a blast. So, this move from general farm equipment to horse trailers was a very fun transition for me. In 1995 we split the business between grass sprigging and farming equipment, which included the horse trailers.

Not long after that, in 1997, we began manufacturing Double D Trailers. It was official: I was all in when it came to horse trailers, and I've never looked back.

Thinking back, that first little tobacco, corn, and bean farm paved the way to many thriving businesses for my family.

*My siblings (from left to right)
Brad, Bartley, and Blair*

To this day, Uncle Doug and his son Canyon own the still successful "Heath Grass Sprigging." My cousin Cierra and her husband Josh own our old retail store, now named H&H Farm Supply. Dad and I stayed in the horse trailer manufacturing business. In 2007 Dad passed away, and my brother Bartley and I continued manufacturing trailers. Bartley and I were partners for many years, until he eventually launched a successful occupational and speech therapy business with my sister Blair.

The Double D Trailers operations team (from left to right: my daughter Brook, my son-in-law Kalib, and me, Brad Heath).

Today, I work alongside my son-in-law Kalib and my oldest daughter Brook. We continue to produce safe, quality, custom-built horse trailers. It's a lot of hard work, but it's a wonderful life.

The Importance of Choosing the Right Horse Trailer

When it comes to the equestrian lifestyle, the importance of selecting the right horse trailer cannot be overstated. A horse trailer is more than just a vehicle for transporting your horse; it is a crucial component of your horse's safety, your safety, and your peace of mind. Making the right choice is about understanding and aligning the needs of your horse with your personal requirements and the diverse options available in the market.

Your horse's experience in the trailer should be as stress-free and comfortable as possible. The right trailer ensures your horse is transported safely and arrives at the destination calm and ready. Factors like ventilation, space, loading style, and suspension play a vital role in your horse's comfort and safety during transit. These aspects become even *more* crucial for longer journeys or when transporting multiple horses.

For the owner, the right trailer brings a sense of confidence and ease. It matches your towing vehicle's capabilities, fits within your budget, and suits your specific equestrian activities — shows, races, trail riding, veterinary visits, whatever it may be. It also means *less* time and money spent on maintenance and repairs, thanks to better build quality and customized features for your usage.

Moreover, the right horse trailer is a reflection of *your* commitment to your horse's well-being — including both their physical and mental health. It demonstrates your responsibility as a horse owner to provide a safe and comfortable environment, not just in the stable but also on the road.

In this guide, **you'll discover exactly what it means to choose the right horse trailer**. From understanding the different types of trailers available to recognizing the key features that matter most, you'll gain the knowledge and insights you need to make an informed decision. A decision that ensures the safety, comfort, and happiness of your equine companion and adds to the joy and ease of your equestrian adventures.

Overview of This Writing

As we embark on this journey together, I want to assure you of one thing: **this is not a sales pitch for Double D Trailers, nor am I here as a salesman.**

Quite honestly, I have a strong dislike for sales people (sorry if you are a salesperson) and do not consider myself to be one. My primary aim is to share knowledge and insights gathered over years of experience in the horse trailer industry. This book is written with a singular purpose: to inform and equip equestrians with the essential knowledge they need to make informed decisions about horse trailers.

In this guide, we'll explore together various aspects of horse trailers that are crucial for every horse owner to understand. We'll begin by dissecting the different types of trailers available and the unique benefits and considerations of each. Whether you're considering a bumper pull or a gooseneck, a trailer with living quarters, or a more basic model, you'll find detailed insights to guide your decision.

Safety is the most important thing when it comes to transporting our equine partners, and we'll give this topic the attention it deserves. From towing safety to the features that ensure your horse's security and comfort during travel, it's all covered. We'll also talk about maintenance, providing practical advice on keeping your trailer in top condition — vital for the safety and longevity of your investment.

Understanding the legal and compliance aspects of owning and using a horse trailer is also critical. We'll navigate through the often-complex terrain of registration, insurance, and legal requirements, simplifying these topics to make them easily understandable.

For those in the market for a new or used trailer, the buying guide section will be invaluable. It's packed with tips on setting a budget, what to look for during inspections, and how to navigate the purchasing process.

I'll also tackle topics like horse comfort and welfare during transit, storage and security of your trailer, and even share real-life stories and case studies to bring these concepts to life. Throughout, my goal is to provide you with unbiased, comprehensive information, empowering you to make the best choices for you and your horse.

This book is a labor of love, born from a desire to contribute positively to the horse community. I sincerely hope that the knowledge shared here enriches your equestrian journey, enhancing not only your understanding of horse trailers but also your overall experience in the wonderful world of horse ownership.

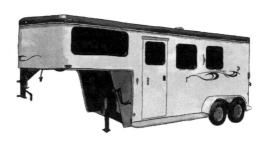

Chapter 1
The Anatomy of a Horse Trailer

Materials and methods matter — big time!

Just think back to the story of the three little pigs. The pigs who built their houses from straw and sticks didn't stand a chance when the big bad wolf came to blow them down. The third pig, though, built his house of brick and mortar. And he stayed safe.

That same mindset of **using the right materials and methods for safety** needs to remain strong in your mind when you consider your horse trailer. There are many brands on the market who cut corners when it comes to safety — resulting in a trailer that is too hot, too loud, too confined, or too weak to stand the rigors of regular use.

In this chapter, you'll gain the fundamental knowledge of horse trailer construction. You'll quickly realize that the choice of materials and configurations directly impacts the trailer's functionality and performance. As we move forward together, keep these foundational elements in mind. These are the building blocks upon which safe, efficient, and comfortable horse transportation is built. Understanding them is key to making the best choices for your horse transportation needs.

Horse Trailer Construction: Materials and Methods

In the world of horse trailers, construction is — quite literally — what makes or breaks a horse trailer. It affects everything, especially durability and safety.

The primary materials builders use to make horse trailers include steel, aluminum, composite materials, and, more recently, 3D printed products. Each of these materials and methods has its unique benefits and drawbacks.

STEEL TRAILERS

Steel is broadly available, lower cost, strong and durable — making it a traditional choice for trailer manufacturing. Back in the day when I started building horse trailers, steel was our go-to material.

As a new manufacturer, it was a low barrier to entry as far as facility and equipment required. We only needed to purchase welding machines, a large shear to cut sheet metal, a plasma torch to cut window holes, a band saw to chop tubing, and an ironworker for specialized parts. And of course, a very large paint booth to paint entire trailers. Since it's so widely available and easy to use, steel is a common choice among manufacturers.

The very first trailer factory for Double D Trailers is shown above. The property started as a Western Auto retail store. After we purchased it, we added two new buildings to the site. We could produce around 200 trailers per year from this facility.

An aerial view of our very first trailer factory in Pink Hill, North Carolina.

Why Steel Has A Bad Rap

A lot of folks tend to freak out a little when you mention "steel horse trailers." Images of rusty, heavy, steel machines might come to mind.

"*Oh no, I don't want a rusty, million-pound trailer!*"

Back in the late '70s and even through the early '90s, that was probably the case. Sealants, primers, and paints were not nearly as protective as they are today. Not to mention, a lot of manufacturers were simply cranking trailers out as fast as they could — without correctly preparing the metal. As a result, the frame or structure of the trailer didn't rust out, but the thin sheet metal did (and that's the part that shows the most). That's why, in the early days of horse trailers, steel earned a reputation of being subpar.

A Rust-Proof Option

When we started manufacturing in 1997, there were many more solutions for durability. Instead of using regular cold roll sheet metal, I used a material called Galvanneal. It's basically galvanized sheet metal made for painting — and it doesn't rust. We coined it as "Galvalite" and advertised it as "No Rust Galvalite."

We, along with many other manufacturers, actually use it today for the interior walls of the horse area due to its superior strength and durability. It's also the same or similar material used in the beds of pickup trucks. The only difference is the shape — we would purchase the sheets flat instead of the ribbed shape for truck beds.

Steel Trailer Manufacturing

The key to building a solid, durable steel trailer isn't rocket science. We quickly figured out that if we used galvanized sheet metal, steel tubes for the structure, and painted with high-quality primer and paint, the trailer held up very well long-term.

Another vital factor for steel trailers is caulking the seams. Think about this: If you weld two pieces of raw metal together (for example, tubing and sheet metal), how can you paint in between them? Well, you can't. Moisture gets in between the unpainted areas and causes the dreaded and dangerous rusting. The only way to avoid this problem is sealing every single seam on the trailer inside and out. By preventing moisture from getting in between the unpainted areas, it virtually eliminates rust.

Fast forward to 2025 when this book was written and a lot of manufacturers continue to use similar construction methods. One example is Trails West. They use galvanized sheet metal to build trailers known for being durable and having a decent value. Another company, Hawk Trailers, uses a galvanized steel frame and combination of aluminum sheets and galvanized sheets. This style makes the trailers very strong in high-stress situations like getting rear-ended or sideswiped, or when an unruly horse spooks. Another example is Logan Coach in Utah; they also build using various forms of steel and galvanized steel.

Today, I often see steel frame galvanized sheet metal Double D Trailers built in the early 2000s for sale. They're built solid, and they still look good.

This Double D Trailer was built in the early 2000s and was recently listed for sale. Because of its construction using a steel frame and galvanized sheet metal, the trailer is still in wonderful shape.

It's surprising how well they've endured over the years and, to be honest, sometimes I wish we continued to build using that method! It was very cost effective, and the trailers are strong, durable, and they get the job done. I have no problem recommending a well-constructed steel/galvanized trailer that uses the correct metal-prepping methods to prevent long-term major corrosion.

And here's the truth: there are always small spots where rust can occur; but it isn't a bad thing, so don't be alarmed. As long as your trailer has a solid build that prevents dangerous corrosion, you'll be just fine with a little rust.

But Isn't Steel Heavy?

Many people are concerned with the weight of their trailer, and rightly so. But the idea that steel is very heavy... Well, it isn't necessarily true. What I've learned over the years is this: a well-built trailer with a steel frame, insulation, and double walls will weigh within 10% of what a well-built aluminum trailer (also insulated and double walled) will weigh.

Steel *does* weigh more than aluminum, but it takes a lot more aluminum to get the strength necessary for a safe trailer. So, when it's all said and done, you ultimately end up adding almost all the weight back in an aluminum trailer.

At the end of the day, if a trailer is *much* lighter in weight — unless it was built using futuristic materials such as carbon fiber — it simply means the builder used thinner materials with less strength, cutting corners somewhere to save on weight (and cost).

My favorite steel construction style is first, welding the frame together, then priming and painting the frame to help eliminate corrosion, and finally, attaching the sheets or skin using 3M VHB tape.

This method is the strongest in my opinion, as the 3M tape provides a watertight barrier — eliminating the "metal on metal" rattle. Many builders today use the 3M VHB chemical bonding technology. They call it tape because it comes in a roll, but it's far from what you would expect. What really happens is a chemical process that literally merges the two pieces of material together as one.

(More on that when we get to the "exterior" skin section.)

I've found in the horse trailer industry, **you truly get what you pay for.** With modern methods of managing weight and controlling rust, today's steel has come a long way compared to the steel of the pre-2000s. In many cases, it can be an excellent and very safe option for your horses.

ALUMINUM TRAILERS

In the late 1970s and early '80s, steel was the primary material for horse trailer construction. At the time it was heavy, cheap, and would definitely rust. Then, along came aluminum, promising to solve all the steel trailer woes.

Aluminum was much more expensive, and the higher price point gave it a higher perceived value. "Cheap steel trailers must be junk! Aluminum is much better!" Or so many consumers thought. Advertised as lightweight, non-rusting, and super strong, aluminum trailers started to sell.

Today, aluminum is the most common material for horse trailer construction. But these trailers are much different than the early aluminum trailers.

How Aluminum Trailers Are Made

It's fascinating how aluminum trailers are made, especially when you compare them to steel. With steel, you simply order angle, tubing, and sheet metal as ready-made parts and weld it all together. You paint, and then you're done!

With aluminum, there are hundreds of small, intricate parts with various shapes made by using dies. I visited an aluminum manufacturing plant and saw firsthand how they make these small pieces.

First, they take what's called a **billet** — a semi-finished piece of aluminum in the shape of a long light pole, around 8-10 inches in diameter. This is what they use to achieve all the different shapes required to build aluminum horse trailers. Next, the mill lays the billet on a conveyor roller and a huge press pushes it through an extruder. Then, the extruder heats the aluminum to where it can be shaped and presses it through a die. Finally, it comes out on the other side in whatever shape the die was made.

In other words, it's just like Play-Doh. You press it through a hole and it comes out in the shape you want.

Most manufacturers have their own dies and shapes and few are the same among different manufacturers. That's why aluminum trailer repair parts often have to be purchased from the original manufacturer (assuming they have the shape available in current production). With steel, parts are much easier to find — it's likely any local steel supplier will have exactly what you need.

Aluminum billets like these provide the raw material for aluminum trailers. The billets are heated until they become malleable and pushed through a metal extruder to form shapes. It works just like your Play-Doh from childhood.

Building an aluminum trailer is basically just assembling a lot of shapes designed to fit together, then welding. A lot of welding. And that's where you get into trouble. Typically, the weld itself is the weak point and most often where cracking or breaking will occur.

Aluminum is a malleable material (think of a tin can), but when you make it thick, it becomes strong. Steel is forgiving in the sense that it will flex many times before it fails — and when it fails, it typically bends rather than breaks. But aluminum isn't as forgiving. There's much less flex, and when it fails it usually snaps, breaks or splinters. The thicker it is, the more brittle it becomes.

This is another good reason to invest in a heavier trailer. More weight means you know it has more material, and will likely withstand a high-stress situation such as an auto accident or spooked horse with a much better outcome.

The Manufacturing Process

The aluminum-trailer manufacturing process generally begins with construction of the aluminum floor. Most are built today with what's called interlocking extruded aluminum. **Extruded** doesn't mean it pokes out of the trailer, it only means it's a certain shape. And **interlocking** means it has tongue and groove boards that fit together.

The aluminum "boards" lock together, and then are welded. Axles are installed with the frame upside down, then flipped over. From there the tubing uprights — similar to vertical boards in the walls of a home — are attached and the structural frame is welded. The exterior skin is typically installed using either mechanical fasteners, glue, or the 3M VHB chemical bonding system more commonly referred to as 3M tape.

This is what a trailer frame looks like before the exterior skin is attached.

The 3M process is the most labor intensive, and probably the most expensive — but it's the most durable, long-lasting, and safe. Not only does the 3M form a watertight barrier and eliminate rattling noises, it also allows the sheet metal to expand and contract freely without binding.

This is especially important for extreme weather situations, because on hot days metal expands, and on cold days, it contracts. If it can't move freely, it will warp. Just walk up to a trailer that uses rivets to secure the sheets, and look down the sidewall. On a hot, sticky, summer day, you'll see the sidewall is wavy. That's because the sheet metal buckled up because the rivets don't allow for flex and movement. The result? Warped trailer walls. (Trailers built with glue have the same issue with warping, plus extra noise from metal-on-metal vibration.)

Floors and Roofs on Aluminum Trailers

Most aluminum horse trailer manufacturers advertise a "solid one piece" or "solid seamless" roof. **Don't be fooled by this marketing tactic.** Always examine the top of a trailer before you purchase it. If there's a mechanical fastener of any sort (like rivets for example), or any type of caulking/sealant around the perimeter, *it isn't solid seamless.*

Imagine a roll of tin foil that's wide enough to cover the width of a horse trailer. If you stretch the tin foil from back to front on a trailer roof, it would technically be one piece. But how will you fasten the sides of the tin foil?

Well, you couldn't — at least not without some type of fastener. Almost every aluminum-built trailer uses mechanical fasteners to attach the tin-foil-style roof material to the sidewalls. This means there *must* be caulking of some sort so it doesn't leak. Over the years, eventually, the sunlight will break down the caulking and leaks will occur. It's not the end of the world and almost any horse trailer repair shop can fix this problem.

However, it often surprises trailer owners, since they were sold the idea of a "solid one piece" aluminum roof. Don't trust the misleading advertisements of "solid one piece" aluminum roofs, because it really isn't the case. Always look on top of the trailer before you purchase to see what type of roof it really is.

(Please note that a fiber composite roof made of fiberglass — like a boat — CAN be made of a single piece without seams or leaks. There is no perimeter seam to maintain or caulk with fiber composite. But, we'll get to that more later in the book.)

Aluminum Trailer Weight

Not all aluminum trailers weigh the same. In aluminum trailers, the heavier the better, since weight often directly correlates with strength. Often to save on weight and cost, a manufacturer may use smaller, thinner materials, since you can't see the thickness of the tubing from the outside.

A 1 x 2" piece of tubing used to construct a divider may be very thin and lightweight (but lack strength) or very thick and heavy and be considerably stronger. For this reason, especially in aluminum trailers, **the heavier the better**. More weight means a stronger and safer trailer. Again, unless it's built with super strong, lightweight carbon fiber, I worry about the safety of the extremely light trailers, especially if they get in a high-stress situation.

Three Things to Consider with All-Aluminum Construction

Most aluminum trailers really do only use aluminum in construction (with the exception of the axles, jack, and the coupler). Almost every other component is aluminum.

While this is a valid construction technique, there are a few things to consider.

First, aluminum gets hot. It's an excellent conductor of heat — which is why it's used to make cookware and solar panels. When you stretch that tin-foil-style shiny aluminum over the roof of a trailer in direct sunlight, *you can literally bake the horse.*

I did a test one time with a thermometer on an uninsulated aluminum roof, which is the way most builders make them. The results were no surprise; the aluminum got hot — so hot I couldn't touch it with my hand — and the inside surface of the horse area roof temperature hit 148 degrees.

For this reason, *insist* on an insulated roof! Many horse owners are worried about air flow more than temperature. While air flow is important, the comfort of the horse has more to do with what material the trailer is made of, rather than how large the windows are. As I was writing this book I received an email from a horse owner whose horse fell down in a trailer after touching a very hot surface and panicking.

> Mikki S. says: *In my horse's attempt to get away, he went down. Despite wearing a leather halter and it being tied to nothing broken. When I was cleaning it, I hit the outside wall with my shoulder blade — it felt like I had hit a branding iron!*

It's much better to transport your horse in a quiet, insulated trailer, than a noisy, boiling hot trailer with no insulation. When trailers are built with the correct material, it will be a comfortable ride even with minimal airflow.

Second, think about the flooring of an aluminum horse trailer. Asphalt can get as hot at 160 degrees on a sunny day, and can be from 25 to 50 degrees hotter than the air temperature. Since horse trailers are built low to the ground, that hot asphalt transfers up to the aluminum flooring of an all-aluminum horse trailer.

Remember aluminum's excellent conductivity properties? That comes into play here. Of all the available flooring materials available today, **aluminum seems to transfer *more* heat, *more* noise, and *more* vibration back to the horse's feet and legs than any other material.** Sometimes I simply scratch my head and ask, "*Why are builders still doing this?*"

Now I'm not knocking aluminum trailers, nor trying to discourage you from purchasing one. But if possible, **choose a flooring type that's not aluminum.**

If nothing else is available, make sure you at least have insulation material underneath the rubber mats on your trailer floor. This alleviates the heat and vibration problem with aluminum flooring. The insulation I'm referring to is a 1-inch-thick piece of foam that is laid on top of the floor, unsecured, with the rubber mat on top. You could easily drag it out with the mat when hosing the trailer and allow it to dry before replacing it.

Last thing to consider: Aluminum and horse urine do not mix very well. Aluminum doesn't go well with moisture over a long period.

Once, a woman traded in her aluminum trailer for a new trailer we built for her. We delivered her new trailer and brought her old one back to the factory. When I went to take pictures of the trailer to post for sale on our website,

I pulled the mats back and could see the ground through the aluminum flooring. It had literally rusted through.

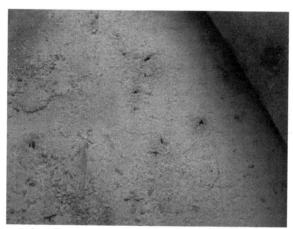

The floors on this aluminum floored trailer had rusted through because of the horse urine that seeped past the rubber mats. This severely weakens the floor and poses a huge safety risk!

Most folks tend to think aluminum doesn't rust, but that isn't true. As you can see from the photo, aluminum oxidizes. The rust is white, rather than red like rusting steel, but it's rust nonetheless.

If you have an aluminum floor, *please* make sure you remove the rubber mats frequently and thoroughly clean the floor. Allow it to dry, then pull the mats back in. Of course, if you have the insulation and mats it's a bit of a pain to move all of it, but it's necessary to preserve the life of the trailer.

Since aluminum has the potential to oxidize with trapped moisture or other harsh chemicals (like horse urine), I generally recommend against any sort of floor "coating" on top of an aluminum floor. A coating is something that adheres directly to your floor and cannot be removed for cleaning.

Yes, I know that there are a lot out there, and many folks have had success with those long-term. However, if just one area of coating fails, moisture or urine can begin to seep underneath the coating, on top of the aluminum. And your trailer floor can end up looking like the one in the photo. If that happens, your floor would rot or rust out and you would never know — until suddenly your horse falls through. That's why it's best to avoid floor coatings on aluminum.

3D PRINTING TECHNOLOGIES

The 3D printing industry, also called additive manufacturing, is expected to reach a market value of 106 billion by 2030 — an insane growth rate! It's a rapidly changing technology that promises to solve a lot of problems. From healthcare to aerospace, to the auto industry and of course, horse trailer manufacturing, 3D printing is an emerging trend across all forms of manufacturing. It allows for complex parts or shapes to be manufactured easily and customized.

How 3D Printed Products Are Made

The process itself sounds simple. The most common method begins with plastic pellets being fed into an extruder. A robotic arm melts the plastic and pushes it through the print head, which basically squirts a bead of material one layer at a time. One layer stacks on top of another as the plastic cools and begins to harden.

There are printers available for printing steel, cement, plastics and fibers of all sorts. The good thing about additive manufacturing is you can change the formula of your print material based on your needs. If you are making a horse trailer window, for example, and using clear plastic as your material, you could easily add some UV inhibitor in the formula to reflect UV and create stronger and more specialized windows for your horse trailer.

Experimenting with 3D Printing Technologies and Horse Trailers

At the time of this writing, Double D Trailers has printed a half-scale horse trailer prototype using a robotic arm.

We made it using polycarbonate and carbon fiber and are working on a full-scale prototype.

Our goal is to 3D print 95% of the components in house, beginning with a one piece full structure, then printing doors, hinges, and ramps which will be installed and fitted. Dividers, vents, windows, doors — pretty much anything on the trailer can be 3D printed (with the exception of tires and axles).

3D printing could have a bright future for the horse trailer industry. Even if it isn't viable for printing the structure of the trailer, it could be very useful for building other parts. I imagine many manufacturers might eventually install their own robotic arms and printers for making parts. This would allow them to create their very own specialized designs — say, windows in a shape, size, and style that isn't currently available anywhere else.

Only time will tell whether or not 3D printing will become a viable method for building entire horse trailers in the future. It will be interesting to see how the industry develops, and if the required safety aspect, strength, and durability can be achieved using this manufacturing process.

Until that time comes, the top trailer brands rely on this last manufacturing process for the most durability and safety...

Composite Material Horse Trailers

Composite simply means a solid material made from two or more materials with different properties.

For example, some trailer manufacturers use a fiberglass roof which is a combination of glass fibers, resin, and other materials. That's a composite material, and a very good choice for horse trailer roofs.

This style of roof is made in a mold (similar to a fiberglass boat). It's one piece, and it doesn't leak. Unlike aluminum roofs, the fiberglass roof is the only one I am aware of that truthfully can be advertised as "solid seamless." Earlier we discussed roof seams and sealants and how aluminum roofs are constructed. The fiberglass roof is a much more efficient roof style, plus, fiberglass is an excellent insulator so it has some immediate benefits as far as temperature control.

In terms of structural framing, there are also some great composite material choices. However, manufacturing of some composite materials is a highly complex process and requires specialized equipment and knowledge. That's why not all trailer brands offer it.

For example, if you take a piece of cold roll steel tubing, add zinc, and put it under intense heat, you'll end up with a material that's stronger than regular steel since the heat tempers the metal and adds strength. The newly formed steel / zinc composite has excellent anti-corrosion properties.

Several manufacturers use similar styles of this material — Hawk, EquiSpirit, Logan Coach, Double D Trailers and Trails West, just to name a few. This composite seems to provide the best of both worlds in that you have the strength of steel with the anti-rusting properties and weight savings of aluminum.

For horse trailers, composite materials are used in many different areas of the final product. The plastics such as door handles, trim, and moldings can be made with composite materials. The 3M VHB tape is also another great example; it's made from an acrylic foam adhesive with viscoelastic properties.

All in all, composite materials offer a great alternative to pure steel or aluminum designs. That's why it's been my material of choice for the last decade.

Why Even Bother with Composite Materials?

Many (if not most) trailer manufacturers are very slow to change or adapt to newer technologies. Often the mindset is, "if it isn't broken don't fix it." It's easier to do what you've always done, rather than trying new things. Especially in manufacturing, making changes in design can be costly and requires a learning curve for workers.

For example, most trailer builders have their entire factory set up for using only aluminum to build the structure. If they were to make a major change in their building material or style, it would potentially require more factory space, more suppliers, new tools and/or dies, and training of specialized labor. This doesn't even include the new product testing that would be needed before offering it to the public.

Often, all of these new technologies actually slow down the manufacturing process, so there's additional cost for labor and overhead. Then, there are always failures in new designs so the cost of future warranties has to be considered combined with negative customer experience if yours happens to break.

All of this "new, new, new" costs a lot of money, so many brands resist making any major changes to their products — even when other methods have been proven to be more durable or safer.

Folks often ask me, "Well if this material is better why isn't everyone using it?" Most often it comes back to the mindset I mentioned: what we are doing is working, and it will cost too much to try and change it. This isn't true with all manufacturers and it's exciting to watch companies in our industry try and innovate.

Brad's Trailer Tips & Takeaways:

- The idea that steel trailers are *much* heavier than aluminum trailers is a myth. Usually, aluminum trailer manufacturers have to add much more metal to make the trailers safe and durable. In the end, this extra layering makes them very comparable in weight to steel trailers.

- Beware of "solid one piece" or "solid seamless" aluminum roofs. Most are not what they claim to be — and they often use mechanical fasteners that rattle and caulking around the edges that eventually lead to decay and leaks.

- Aluminum materials transfer more heat, more noise, and more vibration back to the horse's feet and legs than any other material. Aluminum is an excellent conductor of heat and trailers made from this material can get *very* hot.

- Do NOT choose aluminum flooring for your horse trailer. Even when paired with rubber mats, aluminum floors can oxidize, weaken, and lead to potential dangers.

- When choosing a trailer, always buy from a reputable company. Look for companies that are innovating — ask specifically what improvements and changes they've made in the last five years.

- Look for trailers that are built using a combination of materials rather than all steel or all aluminum.

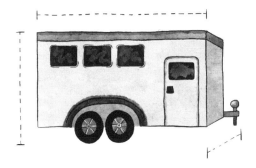

Chapter 2
Understanding Trailer Configurations & Their Purposes

Basic Configurations

The best type of trailer configuration largely depends on you. In other words, how you plan to use your trailer will help you decide whether you need a three-horse, four-horse, living quarters, or even space for something odd like a canoe! (Yes, I once designed a trailer with space for a canoe inside.)

For instance, Cybele G. of New Mexico purchased a trailer from us so she could travel with her mom. She wanted a small weekender package with just enough space for them to do small shows and mother-daughter rides.

Then, Stephanie B. of Idaho wanted a three-horse bumper pull reverse load specifically so she could travel the circuit with her prized show horse. Robin F. and her husband from Nevado wanted a reverse-load living quarters trailer which was perfect for their dream of traveling coast to coast.

Sure, choosing the correct layout, configuration, and style for your trailer can be overwhelming. After all, every horse owner is different. Trailers are not a "one size fits all."

However, there is one important question you can ask yourself to quickly determine which style may be best suited for your specific needs:

How many horses do you need to trailer?

I've asked this question thousands of times over the years, and the most popular response is two to three. I've never really understood that response though. If you need to only haul two horses, you will not want to drag around the extra length of a three horse trailer (not to mention the additional cost and extra weight). But if you need to haul three horses, a two-horse trailer isn't going to get the job done. Three full-size horses will **not** fit in a two-horse trailer, so it's important to consider your long-term goals and the maximum number of horses you plan to haul.

Despite the somewhat confusing response, let's take a look at some different configurations you'll find in the horse trailer market.

BUMPER PULL TRAILERS

The bumper pull trailer is a tried and tested configuration that has stood the test of time. As the name implies, this type of trailer hooks directly to a hitch located on the bumper of your tow vehicle. Horse owners love this configuration because it offers a quick "hitch and go" option.

Two-Horse Bumper Pull

If you only need to haul two horses, and you do **NOT** need camping or overnight amenities, then a two-horse bumper pull is the way to go.

Safety Warning: If you need a camping-style trailer with a bathroom, the **only** safe option for a bumper-pull style trailer is a one-horse bumper pull. Anything with full living quarters that hauls two or more horses *should* be in a gooseneck configuration, or else the hauling weight ratio can cause serious accidents.

Now, there are some builders that offer bumper pulls with full living quarters in a two-horse model, but those can be problematic because they overload a tow vehicle with excessive tongue weight. Ask a trailer dealer about this dangerous problem and they might respond: *"We just move the axles farther forward to lighten the tongue weight,"* but this does not solve the problem. In fact, it can create a seesaw effect. This means that if you haul one horse in the back stall, you could cause a **negative** tongue weight, leading to trailer sway, maneuvering difficulty, and dangerous accidents. **Stay away from any bumper pull trailers with full living quarters that are made for more than one horse.**

A two-horse bumper pull has both straight load and slant load models (which we will discuss soon). Many have configurations with front tack rooms — often referred to as dressing rooms or storage rooms — rear tack rooms, side ramp entry and exit, and reverse load configurations.

Do you need a dressing room in your trailer?

Whether you need a dressing room or not depends on how much stuff you need to carry, and whether you have other storage options (like in a large truck or SUV). If more space is needed, a bumper pull with a front dressing room could be a great option for you. Not to mention, if you wanted to rough camp in it overnight, you could definitely do that (the space is large enough for a cot or blow-up mattress).

If you are purchasing a slant load, by design the angled dividers for the horses create wasted space at the front and back of the trailer. For this reason, most slant load builders will utilize the wasted space as a front dressing room and/or rear saddle compartment.

One-Horse Bumper Pull

If you only need a one-horse trailer, there are a few companies that offer those. The companies that offer the best options are EquiSpirit for a straight load and Double D

Trailers for a slant load. One-horse bumper pull trailers are either slant load or straight load.

Slant load trailers are my preference because they allow your horse to easily walk on and walk off during loading and unloading. As long as the rear saddle compartment is out of the way, your horse can easily turn around when unloading so you *never* have to put your horse in reverse. Some horses reverse fine, while others do not (and some even refuse to!). The same holds true for loading: if the rear saddle compartment is out of the way — either collapsed or folded out — the entire back of the trailer is open and available for loading and unloading. It's much more inviting for the horse, and it's safer for the handler, in case your horse panics. This setup gives you more space and more options for getting out of the way.

There are **straight load trailers** available in a one-horse layout as well. While it serves its purpose, it's basically a two-horse straight-load trailer with a wall built down the center. On one side of the trailer you load the horse, and on the other side, you have room for storage and tack.

One downside to this design is that the full height divider wall creates a "hallway" effect, making the trailer much less open and inviting. If you have to lead in your horse, you're sort of trapped while walking in (although there is an escape door at the front). It's also important to note that there are butt and chest bars to contend with in this design, which can be problematic if a horse were to get a leg over or if they tend to kick while you are trying to raise or lower the bar. And finally, during unloading, your horse must back out of these trailers, rather than walk out. Depending on your horse and what loading and unloading techniques they're used to, this could be a challenge.

Three-Horse Bumper Pull

If you need to trailer three horses, I have built a three-horse trailer in a bumper-pull model. This is safe as long as you have an adequately equipped tow vehicle for towing (that's typically the issue with bumper-pull configurations in general). Unfortunately, many people put themselves and their horses in danger by traveling with unbalanced trailer and tow vehicle combinations. More on that later in the "choosing the right vehicle" section.

Three-horse bumper pulls are available in straight load and slant load configurations. A slant load could potentially be more narrow, allowing you to better see the traffic behind you while traveling. A straight load, on the other hand, must be really wide. Just imagine the width requirement for three horses to stand side by side, facing forward. If you were to purchase a straight-load bumper pull in a three-horse model, I would highly recommend a side exit ramp that allows your horse to walk on and off the trailer without having to back up.

Gooseneck Trailers

A gooseneck trailer earns its name from the long section that hangs over the bed of your pickup truck. Different from a bumper-pull trailer, this gooseneck configuration has a connector that hangs down and connects to a hitch mounted in the bed of your truck.

Ideally, if you need to trailer three or more horses, a gooseneck is the best option for you. Again, I'm not saying you *can't* trailer three horses in a bumper-pull model (or perhaps even four), but in order to do that, you need a pretty large and powerful tow vehicle.

When hauling three or more horses, a gooseneck is much more stable than a bumper-pull trailer. Generally speaking, if you have a ¾ ton tow vehicle, it will be able to safely handle hauling a bumper-pull three-horse trailer model.

For horse owners who need a two-horse trailer, but want more space for rough camping, the two-horse gooseneck model is a fantastic option. There is enough space in the gooseneck portion of the trailer (the area that extends over the bed of the truck) to throw in a full-size mattress and sleep comfortably. Plus, most gooseneck trailers have windows on the sides so air can flow through that section of the trailer.

So if you need to rough camp, and a bumper pull doesn't have enough space, a gooseneck is a great solution. If you need to trailer three or more horses, a gooseneck is the way to go in my opinion.

The main drawbacks to a gooseneck trailer are that you must tow with a truck (not an SUV), and have a special hitch installed in the bed of the truck for towing. In addition, the wheelbase (distance from the back tire of the tow vehicle to the front tire of the trailer) may be longer and require you to swing out more when making turns.

LIVING QUARTERS TRAILERS

To tell you the truth, the living quarter business is something I *never* wanted to be in. Back in 1997 when we started building trailers, our original plan was to only offer stock and cattle trailers. Stock trailers are the ones that have slatted sides or air openings, rather than windows. Some of my first horses were hauled in stock trailers, so I was familiar with the design and hauling technique. However, I later realized that stock trailers are great for livestock, but they are *not* necessarily safe for horses. For this reason, we only offer trailers built for horses, and no longer offer livestock trailers.

When we were building those stock trailers years ago, eventually our clients started asking us for horse trailers. So we started to add horse dividers and saddle compartments, and then we enclosed the trailers and added windows as well.

But it wasn't until 2002 that we began building any sort of living quarter trailer. It started with a conversation with a customer who ordered a two-horse gooseneck trailer with a front dressing room — but with a catch. He said the only way he would purchase it was if we finished out the front room.

He wanted it insulated so he could camp in the trailer and perhaps add his own cabinets or plumbing later on. So, that's what we did.

Being a new trailer manufacturer and trying to grow our business, we decided to make the sale and did a very basic finished interior on his trailer. From there, more people started requesting horse trailers with living quarters, and eventually it grew into a full cabinet shop.

Today, most horse trailer dealers represent at least one or more trailer manufacturers that offer living quarters. When I go to shows I always enjoy walking around and looking at all the trailers with living quarters. It's quite mesmerizing.

Several companies build beautiful interiors with decor that wows. It's quite easy to get caught up in the dazzling beauty factor of a trailer's front interior. After all, the front part is where we humans will stay. Among the different brands and styles of living quarters, there are plenty of variances in size and configuration, and also huge variations in quality, fit, finish, and detail.

Once, when visiting a show in Timonium, MD, I saw a beautiful trailer that had been finished by a company called Outlaw Conversions. Of all the living quarter conversions I've ever seen, that one was impressive, and Outlaw made a positive first impression. The color choices, the finish on the cabinet edges and moldings, the use of hide or leather wall coverings — it was eye-catching, to say the least. It was oriented to a western theme, and the attention to detail was obvious as soon as you opened the door.

Other trailers have much less luxurious looks. I've seen living quarters that look like the inside of a mobile home — with fake cabinets and some sort of paneling wall. Now, there's nothing wrong with fake cabinets. In fact, they're actually called laminate and are probably the most common cabinet used in trailers, since they are lighter than full hardwood cabinets and cost less. Many conversion companies use these types of cabinets.

Speaking of conversion companies, I should explain. Years ago, most trailer builders built the metal structure portion of the trailer, then sold it to a dealer. The dealer would then work with a conversion company that handled the installation of the cabinetry, electrical, plumbing, along with all the other amenities you typically see in RVs. While some manufacturers would work directly with a conversion company before selling it to a dealer, others had less communication and connection. The company making the structure of the trailer, the company doing the interiors, and the dealer doing the sales, were often three separate and different companies.

As you can imagine, during the pass-along process it's easy for details to get lost and things to get mixed up. Several manufacturers still use this style today and it can work just fine. Having a builder that's awesome at building the horse trailer portion and working with another company that's really good at doing the human portion is an excellent combination. The key is making sure someone is coordinating all of the details (typically the dealer).

Over the years, a lot of the industry has consolidated, and several trailer manufacturers started doing living quarter conversions in house, rather than using an outside company. For that reason, there are many fewer conversion companies today than ten years ago.

While there are pros and cons of both, at the end of the day the human aspect — the living quarters portion — really just comes down to your personal preference. What looks nice, and what doesn't, along with the reputation of the company you're working with. After all, a warranty is only as good as the person you are buying from.

If you're interested in a horse trailer with living quarters, make sure to look for manufacturers and dealers with excellent reviews. There's a huge variation in living quarters designs and styles, but don't get caught up drooling over the beautiful interiors and forget about the horses. Not all living quarters are built with your horse's safety in mind. The cosmetic beauty of the trailer is nice, but it absolutely needs to be functional, safe, and comfortable for your horses as well.

Specialized Configurations

SLANT LOAD VS. STRAIGHT LOAD

Over the years I've heard comments from clients such as "my trainer says I need a straight load" or "my vet says I need a slant load."

I always respond: "let the trainer train horses, let your vet doctor your horses, and let the trailer builder build the trailer." I'm a guy who likes facts, not opinions. In the horse world, there are plenty of opinions. "Advisers" typically throw out their opinion whenever they can, but that doesn't mean it's factual.

Years ago, when building and selling in Pink Hill, NC, a husband and wife came to look at our inventory, and they brought along their "trusted" advisor. I started showing them around the store, but to my surprise, their adviser had an opinion about every single product I showed them. His word was gospel, even though his "trusted" opinion actually contradicted a lot of factual information. My tolerance level for a "know-it-all" when they truly do not know what they are talking about is very, very low. After almost 20 minutes, I couldn't take it any longer. I pretended I had a call to take in the office up front and walked away for the three of them to hash it out. I did eventually make a sale to the couple — but only after they returned *without* their lovely, highly one-sided, opinionated adviser. Point being: If you aren't spending your own money, keep your opinion to yourself (*especially* if it's not factual!).

STRAIGHT VS. SLANT: THE SIMPLE FACTS

Early two-horse trailers from the '70s were built as straight loads. Later on, handlers wanted to haul three or four horses, so they developed head to head layouts. These were — and still are — very long, tongue-heavy trailers that are a bit difficult to maneuver (due to the long wheelbase). For example, in a four-horse head-to-head trailer, the horse area alone is 23 feet — not counting any space for tack (which is normally at least an additional four feet). This puts the overall trailer length at 34.5 feet — about as long as a telephone pole.

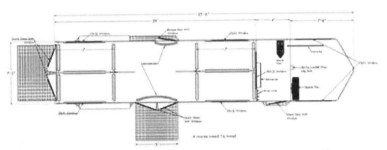

This is a classic four-horse head to head trailer. Two horses would face forward and two horses would face backward with a center aisle way.

The advantage of a head-to-head layout is that you have independent access to each horse. The front horses actually travel facing backwards, and the back horses travel facing forward so they are facing each other. There's a side ramp in between the front and back stalls which is the entry and exit. If you have a horse that doesn't like to back up, hauling him in the front stall could be problematic.

Fact #1: Slant load trailers are usually shorter than straight loads.

To save on trailer weight and length, slant loads were developed as sort of an afterthought. When you haul four horses in a slant, the horse area is only around 17 to 18 feet, compared to 23 feet on the head-to-head layout. The slant load design best utilizes the trailer space and saves you money and fuel (since you're not hauling an excessively large trailer).

Fact #2: Some slant load trailers sometimes only fit smaller horses.

Earlier slant loads (and even a lot of today's slant loads) for whatever reason will only fit smaller horses (usually up to 15.3 hand range). In part, this has given slant loads a bad reputation; many horse owners complain: "My warmblood just won't fit in a slant," or "I can't access all of my horses in a slant without unloading the others first."

These are true statements, to some degree, but once again, horse trailers are not a one-size-fits-all. The fact that your Warmblood will not fit in a slant load trailer has nothing to do with it being a "slant" configuration; it only means the builder of your trailer designed the stalls to fit smaller horses and not Warmbloods.

Fact #3: Research suggests horses haul better in a rear-facing position.

As far as easy access to your horses goes, there are plenty of builders that offer a three-horse slant with a double side ramp, which allows you to access each horse independently. Some configurations even allow you to haul forward or reverse facing.

Research suggests horses haul with less stress in a rear-facing position. I've never actually asked a horse what they prefer, but I do know that if you haul a horse untethered in an open box stall trailer, **almost always the horse will turn at a slant, facing away from the direction of travel.** There are plenty of opinions as to why, but I won't get into those. I stick only with the facts.

A Note about Reverse Load Models

One of the biggest trends I've seen in recent years are reverse load designs. More and more manufacturers have started offering some version of a reverse load configuration. Some are built with horse and handler safety in mind, while others have dangerous design flaws that can put you and your horse at risk. Beware of poorly designed reverse load trailers and always do your research before you buy.

So the question is: *Do horses haul in a straight or slant better?*

Well, let's start with your horse's balance. In a straight load trailer, your horse will brace himself using both front legs and rear legs. While accelerating and braking, the momentum of shifting back and forth to maintain balance will allow your horse to evenly distribute their weight. Of course, when turning or going around curves, there is some side to side force, in which case it wouldn't be evenly distributed.

In a slant load, horses tend to exert slightly more pressure on one of the front legs and the opposite rear leg, rather than both equally. For example, in a forward facing position, your horse may shift on the right front and left rear for balance. A lot of trainers say that for this reason, a horse can arrive at a show and have a lame leg, but after listening to client feedback over the years, we've found that to be untrue for well-designed slant trailers.

People who like slants swear their horses balance better, and load and unload more easily. Typically, in a slant load the horse can walk in, turn around, and walk out, whereas in a straight load, you may have to walk in, and back out (depending on the configuration). People who like straight loads swear their horse doesn't travel well in a slant, and so the argument continues back and forth.

What model sells more, straight load or slant load?

In the 27+ years I've been in the horse trailer business, I've sold a lot more slant loads than straight loads — in fact, probably around 90% of our sales are slant load trailers, and only 10% straight.

Reverse loads today account for 80% of our sales and in most of the layouts you can access each horse independently. Our clients travel in every state all over the US, some even doing cross-country shows with very expensive 17.3 Warmblood size horses. They rave about how well their horse loads, unloads, and trailers. Recently one happy client told us her $30,000 horse didn't travel well in her straight trailer, so she switched to a reverse load slant configuration — with much better performance and a happier horse as a result.

We've figured out how to build trailers comfortably to fit specific size horses — from small ponies to 18 hand horses — and basically solved a lot of the issues associated with unsafe trailer layouts. Now, this doesn't mean slant loads are better than straight loads, or that straight loads are better than slant loads. Just because your neighbor had a bad experience with one or the other doesn't mean you will.

Many people who have had bad experiences with certain trailer models blame the model, when really, it's the specific design elements that make or break a horse's trailering experience. Perhaps if your neighbor had a trailer designed differently, the outcome would have been better.

Poor lighting, small windows, confined doorways, dangerous rear tacks — there are so many factors that can make loading or unloading problematic (and have nothing to do with whether your trailer is a straight or slant load). If the trailer is designed properly, a horse can safely haul in either one.

There are two keys to purchasing a trailer: First, make sure it's designed to fit the size of your horses, and second, choose builders that put horse and handler safety as their top priority.

Tip: If you are looking at a slant load trailer and it has a rear saddle compartment, make sure the compartment can be moved out of the way in case you have a difficult loader. A lot of horses do not like to load through a narrow doorway, so look for designs where the entire back of the trailer can be opened up for maximum loading space. This will make life better for your horse, and keep both you and your horse safe during the loading and unloading process.

Years ago, in 1998, I sold a three-horse slant with a rear tack to a customer. Her horses were self loaders and she had a stationary rear tack compartment. A stationary rear tack is built into the trailer and cannot be moved. It also means you as a handler can't access your horse's head in the last stall when standing inside the trailer, since the tack area is in the way. This horse handler stuck her arm through the slatted trailer side to attach the horse tie, and in that very moment, her horse reared back . . . and snapped her arm! Ouch. Needless to say, we needed a new and safer solution. Many manufacturers offer a collapsible rear tack where the walls will fold out of the way for loading. However, this isn't practical, as you literally have to unload the entire saddle compartment before you can collapse it. Quite annoying! Our solution is we got rid of the dangerous rear saddle compartments and created our SafeTack© saddle compartment, safer both for horses and their handlers.

Tip: When looking at a straight load trailer, pay special attention to the butt and chest bars. These can cause dangerous problems for your horse if they are not properly designed. The bottom line is: make sure that if a horse gets a leg over, you can remove the pin from the bar **even with the weight of the horse on it**. This will allow the bar to move down and out of the way. Otherwise, getting a leg back over a bar could be a real nightmare. There are plenty of builders, such as EquiSpirit and Double D Trailers, that offer butt and chest bars with the ability to easily remove the pin — even with the weight of the horse on it.

A Warning About Stock Trailers

Stock trailers are typically designed to haul livestock — goats, pigs, cattle, and the like. They have open slatted sides and an open interior, often with only a center gate. Most are **not** designed to safely haul horses.

This doesn't mean you can't haul a horse in a stock trailer, but it could cause some serious injuries. I've seen horses suffer injuries after being thrown down from lack of divider bracing, eye injuries from rock or road debris shooting through the slatted sides, cuts and scrapes from sharp edges, eye trouble from dust blowing around, and broken legs when a horse reared up and poked a leg through the slatted side. My preference is to haul horses in trailers that are specifically designed to safely haul only horses.

Custom Configurations

In today's world of custom manufacturing, modification possibilities are almost endless! You can modify individual stalls for the specific size of your horses, change the height, width, and length of the trailer to fit your tow vehicle, and add personalized storage areas for your specific needs.

However, with a ready-built trailer, you can't change much. Sure, you can add some fans and extra tie loops, but nothing major. For that reason, if you plan on purchasing a trailer on a dealer lot, it may be difficult to find one that fits your specific needs.

If you do find one that works for you, then by all means — buy it! If not, I encourage you to explore having your trailer custom made. "Custom" doesn't necessarily mean it costs a lot more, it just means you get what you want. Many manufacturers offer custom trailers, but not all. Several manufacturers specialize in assembly line production with limited customization, since it's much easier to build the same thing over and over (I like to call these cookie cutter trailers). It's much more difficult to build something with a lot of changes from trailer to trailer. For this reason, it's important to choose a reputable builder known for successfully building custom-built trailers.

Brad's Trailer Tips & Takeaways:

- Bumper pull trailers with full living quarters that are made for *more* than one horse are NOT safe. Only one-horse models have a safe hauling ratio. If you want a living quarters trailer and need to haul more than one horse, a gooseneck trailer configuration is the best option.

- Slant load trailers (especially those with a side door) allow your horse to easily walk on and walk off during loading and unloading, making this process much easier for them and for you.

- There are two keys to purchasing a trailer: First, make sure it's designed to fit the size of your horses, and second, choose builders that put horse and handler safety as their top priority.

- Beware of rear saddle compartments — while everyone loves extra storage space, these built-in designs can narrow the loading space and cause dangerous accidents. Look for designs that keep the loading space wide and clear for your and your horses' safety.

- Pay special attention to the butt and chest bars in a straight load trailer. They must be easily removable, even with the full weight of your horse's leg weighing down on them. If not, dangerous accidents can occur.

- Never haul horses in a stock trailer — these trailers are not designed to haul horses safely.

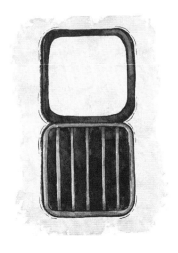

Chapter 3
Design Elements & Horse Trailer Features

One small seed can turn into a beautiful flourishing tree that children can climb, swing from, and have picnics under. But that same small seed — if planted too close to a road or home — could turn into powerful roots that crack sewer pipes, damage your house's foundation, and cause serious problems. The little things make a big difference. And so it is for your horse trailer.

Each little component contributes to the overall functionality, safety, and comfort of your trailer. Understanding these features is fundamental in creating an environment that not only ensures the well-being of your horses but also facilitates ease of use for you as an owner.

In this chapter, I'll take you through the critical design elements and features of horse trailers — everything from windows, roofs, and floors to walls and insulation. Each element plays a special role in creating a horse trailer that's safe and comfortable, both for you and your horse.

Let's Break Down Some Key Trailer Features

DIVIDERS

Different styles of dividers cater to different trailer types. In a straight load trailer, the divider runs parallel to the trailer's sidewalls — front to rear, with horses loaded on either side. Slant load trailers feature angled dividers (the specific angle depends on the manufacturer). Reverse load trailers often utilize a double swinging divider with hinges on both ends, allowing it to pivot in either direction — an absolutely essential feature in slant load trailers with a side ramp. In slant load trailers, a horse's body is supported along the length of the partition, potentially offering greater protection in high-impact scenarios.

Trailer dividers need to be strong. If you get in a rear-end collision, get sideswiped, or if a horse spooks during transit, the divider absorbs the brunt of the impact. In straight load trailers, the chest and butt bars also take up most of the impact — impact that would more than likely cause bruising or serious injury, depending on its severity.

Trailer dividers also need to be functional. Conventional slant load dividers usually have a slam latch that makes it easy to open and close — you don't have to fiddle with pins or worry about small pieces. For double swing dividers, slam latches aren't practical since the divider has to pivot from both ends. Since there's not a good way of manufacturing those with slam latches, most will have pins. It's slightly more cumbersome from a user perspective, but many clients say they aren't too difficult to use and the safety benefit outweighs the negative. The side ramp or reverse load configuration makes this little extra step worth it.

Partition designs also vary, particularly regarding the head stall that separates horses. Many manufacturers offer a solid sheeted head stall, made from materials like steel, galvanized steel, or aluminum, framed in tubing. While this design is cost-effective and quick to install (reducing the cost of the trailer), it limits visibility, light, and airflow, which can create a claustrophobic environment for horses.

This trailer has a solid divider shown in the circle.

Tubular head dividers that allow air and light to pass through reduce claustrophobia and make the trailer much more inviting.

Full-height dividers are another option. These extend almost all the way up to the roof, preventing a horse from getting a leg over the divider. The lower partitions, or stud gates, stop the horse's legs from going under the divider. These designs — when they have a lower partition and are made with tubes — are likely the safest, especially in high-impact situations. If you have full-height dividers and a lower partition, just make sure the tubes up top are close enough together that a foal can't fit a leg through, and the perimeter gaps near the walls and floors are very small. Otherwise, a horse could get a leg stuck in a gap and be severely injured.

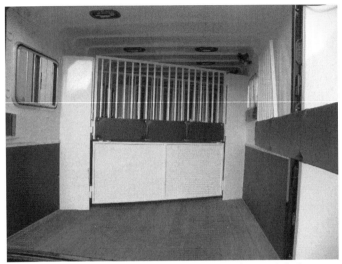

Double swinging full-height divider with lower partition (stud gate).

It's important to note that, unlike automobiles, there's no standardized crash testing for horse trailers. That's why it's crucial to select a manufacturer known for safety and quality. Don't be afraid to ask about the thickness and strength of the materials used, especially since materials used to build dividers vary. If a manufacturer can't provide this information, it might be wise to look elsewhere. It's also easy to compare weights, the more weight, the more material which equals greater safety.

Padding

Padding provides extra cushioning and comfort, especially in high-stress or high-impact situations. Most padding is made from vinyl with foam and a stiff backing. In my experience, black padding tends to show less dirt and wear compared to lighter colors. The choice of adding padding should be based on your preference for safety and comfort.

Surprisingly, many trailers are built without padding in the horse area. And while many buyers and dealers are ultra-focused on the horse's well-being, they sometimes overlook crucial safety aspects. Padded walls, see-through dividers, and functional chest and butt bars are absolutely essential in straight load trailers. These elements are key for ensuring the horse's safety and comfort.

This trailer does not have any padding throughout the entire interior. It also has solid head dividers so horses can't see their neighbors.

However, certain seemingly "ergonomic" designs often put safety second. One example is a design called "two plus one." In this configuration, a horse is placed up front without adequate padding, a divider, or a partition — in the "plus one" area. This seems contradictory to the focus on safety and raises questions about the design methodology.

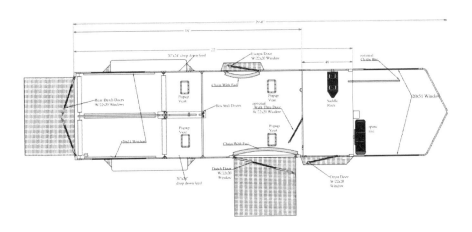

A "2+1" configuration has two horses in the rear of the trailer standing in straight load stalls with a third horse in a box stall at the front.

In my view, when designing or purchasing a safe trailer, it's imperative to ensure that each horse has its own individual stall, equipped with necessary padding. A well-thought-out design should provide equal safety measures for *each* horse, regardless of their position in the trailer. Neglecting these aspects can compromise the safety and comfort of the horses — especially in the "plus one" area. If you have two kids you wouldn't buckle one child in a seatbelt and not the other one!

Windows

In the realm of horse trailers, windows serve two key functions: providing ventilation and allowing light into the trailer. A range of styles are available, with several US manufacturers producing windows that are often interchangeable with those in the RV or camper industry.

One of the larger manufacturers is Statewide Aluminum in Elkhart, Indiana. Statewide Aluminum — along with other similar companies — offers various styles, allowing trailer builders to customize according to specific requirements. I particularly like the drop-down feed window design at a horse's head. It's user-friendly, as you can easily walk up to the side of the trailer, open a latch, and fold the window down. These windows typically feature bars on the inside, keeping your horses safe by preventing them from sticking their heads out. Ideally, the bars and windows should operate independently, as this enhances both safety and functionality.

A drop-down feed window is easy to open from the outside while keeping the horse safely secured with bars. The bars and windows operate independently.

However, a common issue with these drop-down windows is the latching mechanism. It's often not as user-friendly as it could be, especially in designs where the latch is placed too high, making it difficult for a person of average height to reach. Thankfully, some manufacturers have started designing windows with the latch placed in the middle, making it much more accessible (particularly for those of us who are height challenged).

Another option in the market is sliding windows. Instead of folding down, these feature two glass panes, one of which slides over the other, accompanied by bars on the horse area side. These windows have an impressive safety design. If the window is struck by an object, it shatters into tiny, less harmful pieces, rather than dangerous shards of glass (windshields in automobiles have a similar safe design). This design reduces the risk of injury to horses from sharp glass edges.

Some manufacturers that opt for sliding windows rather than drop-down windows sometimes incorporate a small sliding window within a larger door. While this might sound practical, it often results in limited airflow and reduced light penetration — not to mention the added weight and cumbersomeness of the doors. In my experience, this design is less efficient than the mid-latch drop-down windows. These types of windows are cumbersome to use, since opening the bars requires two hands.

When choosing a trailer, it's essential to consider how the windows function, the ease of use of latches, and overall window durability. Pay attention to the windows and do a little testing to see how sturdy they are. From a manufacturing perspective, finding a quality window that seals properly and doesn't leak remains a challenge.

Even high-quality options available today seem to lack the sturdiness of those from a decade or so ago. Windows are problematic because they leak, they freeze up and won't slide, or the rubber trim and sealant pops out. As of this writing, at Double D Trailers, we are working on developing our own window that will be a vast improvement on what's in the market currently.

Exploring Different Types of Roofs, Floors, Walls, and Insulation

Roofs

Horse trailer roofs are one of those things that many buyers don't pay a whole lot of attention to. However, it's one of the most important aspects of the trailer — particularly when it comes to horse comfort and temperature regulation.

There are four primary types of material used for roofing: aluminum, cold roll steel sheet metal, fiber composite, and a combination of steel, aluminum, and insulation.

First, aluminum roofs. These are the most common in horse trailers, primarily due to cost savings and speed of installation. However, it's important to note that while aluminum is excellent for applications like solar panels and cookware (due to its heat conductivity) it may not be the best choice for a horse trailer roof. Despite its widespread use, because aluminum is such a powerful heat conductor, it can significantly impact the internal temperature of your trailer. High interior trailer temperatures can cause dehydration, overheating, and heat stress for your horses during transportation. The bottom line is: **you should not be towing a trailer with a non-insulated aluminum roof. Don't be fooled!**

Some manufacturers advertise aluminum roofs as solid, seamless structures, which is very misleading. During manufacturing, a roll of mill-finish aluminum is stretched across the trailer's length, trimmed, and secured to the sidewall with rivets or screws, which are then sealed. While they may lack seams from front to rear, they **do** have a seam around the perimeter, sealed with roof sealant. This sealant can deteriorate over time due to sunlight exposure, requiring maintenance.

Next, sheet metal roofs, made from 4 x 8 sheets. This style has its advantages, but it also has seams every four feet, which over time require resealing. Interestingly, steel roofs can be painted white, **making them more reflective and efficient in heat management than aluminum.** While not as crucial, adding insulation to this type of roof is also beneficial.

A few years ago, we developed an in-house insulated roof panel, made up of a Galvalite sheet on the bottom side, white aluminum on top, and high-density styrofoam insulation sandwiched in between. This structure created a solid, super-insulated, and forgiving roof. In the case that an unruly horse rears up and hits its head against the roof, the Galvalite sheet on the bottom is strong enough to support the impact yet the insulation in between allows the panel to flex which helps in reducing injury. However, maintenance can become an issue over time due to the seams every four feet and the ongoing need of resealing so we stopped producing that style.

Lastly, fiberglass or fiber composite roofs. Since this material is excellent for insulation — similar to the fiberglass insulation commonly found in the walls of residential homes — it's used by many horse trailer manufacturers. Manufacturers like Hawk Trailers in Wisconsin and Gore Trailers in North Carolina build using fiberglass roofs, along with many others. After looking at numerous materials, **fiberglass stands out as the top choice for climate control and ease of maintenance in horse trailers.**

Fiberglass roofs offer excellent heat reflection and insulation. They're typically painted white and molded like a boat hull, making them genuine one-piece structures. This eliminates the need for seam maintenance and ensures easier long-term upkeep. Since they are truly one piece, you will not have any leaks with a fiberglass roof.

Floors

Proper flooring in horse trailers is extremely important. Floors must withstand horse pawing or stomping, extreme amounts of weight shifting around, and the chemical consequences of horse urine and horse waste. The two most popular materials for flooring are wood and aluminum.

Since we started manufacturing horse trailers in 1997, our standard flooring has been wood, specifically two-inch by eight-inch pressure-treated pine. We install the boards when green and fit them together tightly so there's no gap in between. As the board dries within the trailer, it creates small gaps for airflow — crucial for water escape and floor dryness. Covered with a rubber mat, this setup provides a durable and safe flooring option.

In the past, manufacturers ran boards side to side for cost efficiency, resulting in tongue-and-groove floors with no gaps for moisture escape or drying, leading to quicker deterioration. Today, installing boards lengthways, parallel to the sidewall, without tongue-and-groove joints, is more effective (especially when the wood is pressure-treated). Regular maintenance, including removing the mats, hosing the floor, and drying it thoroughly can significantly extend your wood floor's lifespan and durability.

Aluminum floors are also very common. Typically, they're made either from interlocking extruded aluminum or laid atop I-beams or cross members. While each style has its pros and cons, aluminum transfers more heat, more noise, and more vibration compared to other materials. Properly maintaining your aluminum floor is critical to prevent corrosion, especially from horse urine. Despite its perceived longevity, aluminum requires regular cleaning and drying for long-term durability.

There are some solutions that aim to mitigate aluminum's downsides; one example is coatings that reduce heat transfer. Now, I'm personally not a fan of these because the coating needs to bond. If that bond were to actually separate — or if the human who installed the coating didn't prep the metal properly or just didn't do a good job in one spot — moisture will begin to seep underneath the coating, on top of the aluminum. That moisture would get trapped in between the coating and the aluminum, causing oxidation and rust. Because of this, the floor could actually rust out and a horse could fall through the floor during transit, causing serious injury and a potential traffic accident — and you would never know it until the failure occurred.

That's why I definitely don't recommend coatings of any sort, simply for long-term durability. There are many out there, and a lot of folks have had success with that style. However, I'm just not sure how well those floors are going to hold up in the future as years from now there might be some serious deterioration and dangerous failures. I don't recommend putting yourself and your horses at risk.

One promising horse trailer flooring alternative is Rumber. This material is made from recycled tires — it's two inches thick, eight inches wide, and runs parallel to the trailer's sidewall. Rumber eliminates the need for stall mats and transfers the *least* amount of heat, noise, and vibration. Since it's solid rubber, it's virtually indestructible. I highly recommend it. A lot of manufacturers offer it, and it's not proprietary to any one horse trailer manufacturer, so anyone could install it for you. We install Rumber in approximately 95 percent of the trailers we sell.

Walls and Insulation

WALLS

Horse trailer walls consist of a lower wall (where the horse kicks) and an upper wall, which is the area around the windows to the ceiling. How manufacturers build horse trailer walls varies significantly, and understanding these variations is important for determining the safety and durability of a trailer.

In the simplest form, a single-walled horse trailer is built by covering a skeletal frame with a flat sheet of metal, typically aluminum or steel. This design allows someone inside the trailer to directly touch the exterior skin's inner side. However, this single-layer construction is not without its flaws; the thin metal sheet more than likely would *not* withstand neither the kick of a horse nor the impact of another vehicle in an accident, especially if the upper wall is aluminum. A rearing horse can easily poke a hole through the metal, damaging their delicate legs and the trailer.

To enhance structural integrity and safety, most manufacturers opt for a double or multi-walled construction for the upper wall. This method involves installing an additional protective layer inside the skeleton, usually extending from the lower wall (where the horse kicks) to the roofline. The inside sheet metal can be aluminum as long as there is insulation behind it. That way, if a horse rears up, there's only a minimal risk of injury; the walls are much stronger, which prevents a horse from sticking a leg through the metal.

Using some sort of steel for the inner upper wall (for strength and durability), and aluminum for the exterior wall (with insulation sandwiched in between both) is a great technique. When it comes to materials, manufacturers might use a variety of metals for the outer walls, including standard steel, galvanized metal, or aluminum — all fine options.

When designing the lower wall, it's important to create a wall that's strong yet flexible, since this portion of the wall is nearest to the horse. One common setup is incorporating a steel plate into the lower wall, then covering it with a thick rubber layer to cushion potential impacts. This is used for all the internal wall areas where the horse could kick.

Many trailer designers prefer using thick rubber or poly materials for the inner walls. These materials not only prevent damage from kicks but also provide some flexibility, reducing the risk of injury. Poly materials — composed of a blend of plastic and rubber — are especially valued for their slight give, which can absorb and disperse impact more effectively than rigid materials.

INSULATION

Insulation between the wall layers also plays a key role in absorbing impact, regulating temperature, and reducing noise and vibrations while the trailer is in motion. Regardless of the trailer's brand or manufacturer, without proper insulation, vibrations can be significant — even with a single-walled build. It's simply the nature of the design.

I've ridden in the back of a trailer, and it's incredible just how noisy and shaky it is. Back in the day when we built single-walled trailers, at Christmas we would take several of our church members Christmas caroling in a small neighborhood. Yep, in the back of a horse trailer. Everyone would pile in the back of the trailer to get from house to house. Speeds never exceeded 20 MPH, but I do **not** recommend riding in the back of trailers because *it is dangerous and illegal*. But it was amazing how noisy the trailer was and the amount of shaking we experienced.

To mitigate trailer noise and vibration, the ideal construction would include the skeleton frame, an exterior sheet on the outside, followed by a layer of insulation covering the entire wall section of the horse area, including the doors and the slant wall. Another sheet of material is applied on top, completing what is known as a double-walled trailer. **This construction is crucial for safety.** Even if a horse rears up and strikes the sidewall above the kick lining — possibly near the window area — there is *minimal risk* of a hoof puncturing through.

The same principle applies to the trailer's ceiling. No matter what material you use for your ceiling, other than fiber composite, it should be double-walled and insulated. This not only prevents heat transfer, but it also minimizes damage and injury in case a horse happens to strike its head against the ceiling between structural supports. This ceiling configuration is flexible and absorbs impacts, which protects the ceiling and reduces the risk of injury to the horse.

The Importance of Ventilation and Lighting in Trailer Design

Ventilation

Ventilation is often a primary concern among buyers transporting livestock such as cattle, sheep, and goats in open-sided, slated stock trailers. For horses, however, the need for controlled air and more comfort is **even more crucial.** The safest option for your horse is a fully enclosed horse trailer with windows that not only allow for light, but can also be opened or closed to adjust airflow. Most trailers are equipped with roof vents that help in circulating air while moving.

The determining factor for your trailer's internal temperature is the material used in construction. A single-walled aluminum trailer with a mill finish roof and no insulation can quickly turn into a "microwave box," overheating the horses inside. Materials like aluminum get hot, fast. In contrast, a double-walled construction with insulated walls and ceiling, along with appropriate flooring materials that transfer minimal heat ensure that the horse travels comfortably, even with only a small amount of airflow.

That's why when purchasing a trailer, it's much better to focus on **insulation and controlled airflow** rather than just the number of vents or size of the windows.

Lighting

Lighting also significantly impacts the internal environment of your trailer. Large, easy-to-open windows provide excellent ventilation and make the trailer more inviting during loading, since horses tend to avoid dark, confining spaces.

Regarding artificial lighting, most modern trailers use LED lights, which consume minimal energy. Lights — including specific loading lights — are crucial for night travel. It is important to ensure that the trailer's wiring is done correctly. Manufacturers must use grommets to protect the wires from being cut by sharp metal edges due to vibration. If builders omit this essential step, you could experience electrical short circuits and have to do frequent repairs.

Interior lights not working is actually a common issue. These lights typically operate off the auxiliary circuit from the tow vehicle. However, many vehicle manufacturers don't install the fuse that activates this circuit, requiring owners to do it themselves. To resolve this, owners need to consult their vehicle's operator's manual to locate the fuse block, install the fuse, and activate the auxiliary system.

Brad's Trailer Tips & Takeaways:

- Do not choose a trailer with a non-insulated aluminum roof — aluminum is a powerful heat conductor and these types of roofs can turn your trailer into an oven. A horse who sweats a lot can quickly become dehydrated.

- Coating an aluminum floor can reduce heat transfer, but if not done perfectly, can cause the trailer floor to rust out and lead to a dangerous accident on the road.

- Make sure your trailer is double-walled. Strong, durable walls with sufficient insulation prevent serious injury caused by a horse kicking a leg through the wall.

- Vents and windows are important for your horse's comfort in the trailer, but always focus more on insulation and controlled airflow when looking at potential trailers.

Chapter 4
Trailer Mechanics & Hardware

A woman named Sara was traveling with her two-horse bumper pull trailer through the Great Smoky Mountains, when she suddenly heard a huge "Bang!"

She gripped the steering wheel tightly and gazed into her side mirror to see debris kicking up behind her. Sara looked frantically for a place to pull over but the narrow mountain roads didn't allow for it.

After driving several more miles, and finally finding a safe spot to pull over, Sara got out of her truck to observe the damage. It was a mess. Her trailer's tire had blown, that much was clear. She looked closer to see that the tire had completely come apart during the drive to safety, chewing up her fender and damaging the sheet metal on the trailer's exterior wall.

Thankfully, Sara and her horses were safe. Now, she was just faced with a huge repair bill and massive headache as she worked to change the tire on a narrow mountain road.

My goal with this chapter is to help you avoid ever being in a situation like Sara — one where your trailer fails you midway through a trip. I'll guide you through the vital mechanics and hardware that are essential for the safe and effective operation of your horse trailer.

We'll look at everything from the tires and suspension system that carry you down the road, to the door latches and hinges that secure your precious cargo. Each of these elements plays a crucial role in the overall functionality of your trailer. Understanding these components, along with the warranties that protect them, is fundamental for a safe, efficient, and worry-free journey for both you and your horses.

Tires and Suspension Systems: Choices and Maintenance

When it comes to tires and axles for your horse trailer, there are numerous choices available. There are a plethora of brands of tires, several manufacturers across the globe that produce axles, and of course many companies that make the components that make up those axles, the bearings, and the braking systems. Over the years, we've had the opportunity to use many brands of tires and we've tried quite a couple different axle brands.

For tires, I've always come back to brands that have at least a three-year warranty from the manufacturer — not the manufacturer of the *trailer*, but the manufacturer of the *tire*. If they don't have at least a three-year warranty, I wouldn't buy them.

Many manufacturers will order tires made in China. Now, just because it's manufactured in China doesn't mean it's subpar. Tire manufacturers will often build for many brands of tires, and if they outsource the manufacturing to China (or any other country), those factories will manufacture to the spec of the brand.

For example, lawn mowers usually aren't made by the brand company you see on the machine. Most of them are made by MTD, the largest lawn mower manufacturer in the US. MTD produces machines for more brands than I can count (they even make some John Deere mowers). But not all the lawn mowers are built the same. If you look at the different brands, you'll see that some of the components are common, but many are not. The mowers are built specifically according to the spec requirement of the brand that's selling.

The same is true for tires. If you compare two different tires made in China, one brand may have only a year warranty, whereas another brand may have a warranty that lasts three years or more. We even found a tire company that gives a five-year warranty. Since changing to those, we've had very minimal tire failures.

We get a lot of questions about tires, especially if someone is having a custom trailer built. Many people assume that the heavier the tire, the better. Some people request the heaviest tire possible, or the thickest tire with the most plies, thinking that will last longer and be better able to haul the trailer. But that's just not true. In fact, that's actually not a good way to build a trailer, since you *always* want to make sure the suspension is adequate — and I consider suspensions to include the tires, the rims, and the axles. All of those things must be properly matched to the load being carried, not grossly overrated or underrated.

In other words, if you have a D-Rated tire — which is generally an eight-ply capable of carrying about 2,500 pounds per tire, or around 10,000 pounds total — you wouldn't want to use that tire on a suspension that's capable of carrying 14,000 pounds. **Remember, trailers are only as strong as the weakest link in the equation.** So if you have a weak tire and a strong axle, or vice versa, you could still have a failure within the tire. If you have an axle that's too small and a super heavy or thick tire, then you can have an axle failure. The point being, if the manufacturer of the trailer matches the tire and the entire suspension system to safely carry the load being hauled, that's going to produce the best ride possible.

You may ask, "Well how will I know this information when I'm purchasing a trailer?"

First, identify the empty weight of the trailer. This is the first thing you should calculate when looking for a trailer. There are lots of terms you'll discover, like GVWR and GVW, but don't get confused on those things now. You're just looking for the weight, nothing else.

Now, the actual trailer weight is NOT shown on the VIN sticker or tire placard. The only true method of obtaining a trailer weight is to tow it to a truck scale. Many truck stops have scales for weighing 18-wheelers and any of those will be happy to weigh your trailer.

Next, determine the trailer tongue weight. The tongue weight is the amount of the load that's distributed to your tow vehicle, and not carried by the trailer's suspension. **Tongue weight is actually more important than the trailer weight,** since the "weak link" in a vehicle for towing comes from the payload, which includes the trailer tongue weight.

For example, if you have a three-horse trailer that weighs 5,000 pounds and the average weight of your horses is 1,200 pounds each, plus tack, gear, water, and other accessories, your total weight may be around 9,000 pounds when you add it all up. So you will need a suspension system rated to safely carry a *minimum* of 9,000 pounds, minus the tongue weight of the trailer as that weight is carried by the tow vehicle. If it's a bumper pull, the weight is carried directly on the back bumper/hitch of the vehicle; if it's a gooseneck, the weight is carried in the bed of the truck.

Is Your Suspension System Safe?

In my opinion, when manufacturers list the axles and the tires at a specific rating, that tire and axle will safely carry the advertised load rating. I always like to have a little bit of cushion, just in case you haul more tack and gear. But, going back to our example of the 9,000 pound trailer, *there's absolutely no need* to have a 12,000 or 14,000 pound suspension on a trailer that is only carrying 9,000 pounds when max loaded. And if you have a multi-horse trailer, you must remember that you won't always haul the full capacity. Many times you may only haul one horse or two horses.

Having a suspension system that is too heavy does **not** make your trailer safer. In fact, it means the ride is going to be stiff. You'll have additional shock and bounce on the trailer, which is then transferred back to the horse's feet and legs.

Where Do You Find Important Information About Your Tires?

If you look on the sidewall of the tire, you'll find all of the information you need. First, you'll find a **date code which allows you to decipher when the tire was manufactured.** In the following tire image, the date code is LMLR5107. This means it was manufactured on the 51st week of the year, and the "07" means it was manufactured in 2007.

It's normal to have a tire that was built a year before the trailer was actually purchased. Many times, tires are built overseas, shipped in a container across the ocean, and stored in a manufacturing facility, then finally installed on your trailer. In those cases, the tires are generally indoors and not exposed to sunlight or outdoor elements, so the breakdown of the compound or the rubber itself is minimal. Remember, tires don't *wear out*, they *age out*. We'll discuss that in a moment.

The next thing you need to look for on the tire is the **number of pounds the tires are rated to carry.** It's a very simple equation. Just look at the number stamped on the tire that says what it's rated to haul, and multiply by four (since you'll have four tires on the trailer). That little calculation gives you the capacity of all the tires on your trailer.

Speaking of capacity, it's also important your trailer tows level. Imagine moving a piece of furniture with a friend, maybe a long couch, and one end of the couch is really low, while the other end of the couch is lifted up really high at a tilt. The person on the low end will end up carrying a much greater load than the person on the high end.

The same thing goes for the trailer. You want to make sure that your trailer is as level as possible. If the front end is jacked up, it will shift the additional weight to the back axle and the back tire. Your trailer ride will be more bouncy and will jerk more — and you run the risk of an overload, overheating a tire, and a potential blowout. Avoid that at all costs. Again, the number of plies in a tire is much less important than the weight that the tire is rated to haul. The number of plies will be taken care of based on the weight that it's rated to carry.

The last important piece of information that's written on the sidewall of a tire is **the air pressure, or maximum PSI.** Many tires are rated around 50 pounds, maximum PSI, while others are rated closer to 80. It just depends on the tire brand, the weight it's rated to haul, and the size of the tire.

You'll typically want to look at trailers that have an ST rating on the tire. "ST" simply stands for special trailer. For many years, ST tires were rated at a max speed of 65 MPH, and many today still have the same rating. A few manufacturers have introduced tires with speeds up to 75 MPH, but be sure to check the speed rating on your particular tire brand.

The other type of tire is "LT" or light truck, which is designed for automobiles. The difference between the ST tire and the LT tire is that the special trailer tire has a stiffer sidewall. Think of a horse trailer's height, or an RV which is even taller than a horse trailer. This makes it possible to haul top-heavy loads. When you're rounding curves with a top heavy load you want to make sure that you have a tire that has a sidewall designed so that the tire doesn't roll. A tire without a stiff sidewall will allow the top of the trailer to rock back and forth more, whereas a stiff sidewall tire prevents the top of the trailer from rocking back and forth as much. Less rocking is important for the best ride in a horse trailer.

How Do Trailer Suspension Systems Work?

Your trailer's suspension is made up of axles, springs, dampers, shock absorbers, and other pieces that all work together to safely support the trailer weight and provide a smooth ride for you and your horses.

The largest manufacturer of axles in the US is Dexter Axle Company. We've personally used Dexter since 1997 and they seem to provide the best service when it comes to suspension. Many years ago, Dexter significantly increased their prices, so we decided to try a less expensive suspension.

During that time, I had a client in Texas hauling a three-horse bumper pull trailer from point A to point B. When she started, she had four tires, but when she arrived at point B, she only had three. The whole hub had broken off without her realizing! Thankfully, the tire and the wheel didn't go through someone's windshield and severely injure anyone.

After that, we quickly changed back to Dexter. And we've never had another experience like that since. They're the best in the industry, although today there are more options with good reputations.

If you're looking at horse trailers, always ask the brand of axle that's installed on the trailer and if possible, insist on a Dexter axle. Those seem to have the fewest failures with braking and bearings, much less than other axle manufacturers.

As far as suspension, there are a couple different types on the market. One is **leaf spring**. If you don't know what a leaf spring suspension is, just look behind the tire of your automobile. You'll see springs with a shock. Those components are what absorb the impact as you travel over bumps in the road. For over 15 years, we actually built with the leaf spring suspension. It's reliable, very durable, and works quite well.

Another type of suspension is **rubber torsion.** It's basically a piece of rubber inside of a square tube. Rather than having a leaf spring or a shock that moves as the tire and wheel moves up and down, it simply twists the rubber. The thickness and stiffness of the rubber determines the capacity or the amount of weight it could haul.

Many years ago, Dexter developed their TORFLEX axle. Initially, we didn't jump on the rubber torsion bandwagon because we heard stories of clients who had relatively new trailers with rubber suspensions that wore out really quickly and created a very bouncy ride. A few folks even brought other brands of trailers to us and paid us to remove their

TORFLEX suspension and replace it with a conventional leaf spring. That was more than 20 years ago. Today, Dexter rubber torsion axles seem to be very durable.

In fact, those are the axles we use today. Compared to the leaf spring, the ride is much smoother with the rubber torsion. It costs a little more money but it's worth it in the long run, especially since Dexter also has easier maintenance on their axles now. In years past, you were not able to replace the rubber portion of the axle, and instead had to purchase an entire new axle. Now, with the way they're manufactured, you can easily pull out one wheel or one hub, do whatever maintenance that you need to do, and then put it back together.

The last type of suspension system is **air ride**. I have only installed air ride on less than five trailers in my career, since it is extremely expensive, and very maintenance-heavy. (You can imagine air lines, maintaining pressure, and things of that nature.) It's just not worth the additional money. But if that's a suspension you'd like to explore or you really want, there's certainly nothing wrong with it.

To sum it all up, when it comes to tires and suspension systems, Dexter axles are the way to go. Always identify the weight capacity of the tire and make sure all of the numbers match, and you'll be able to safely carry the load you plan to haul.

Braking Systems

When it comes to braking systems, which are also part of the axle, most trailers are produced with **electric brakes**. Electric braking systems are simple, reliable, and easy to operate.

There are also **hydraulic disc brakes**, which have greater stopping ability. In my experience, the electric braking system has worked just fine; and the additional cost of the hydraulic braking system just isn't warranted.

Sometimes, after delivering a new trailer, clients report issues with wheels slinging grease. This often occurs when the trailer's braking system is set too tight, leading to excessive brake heat and watery grease slinging. Adjusting the trailer's braking system to reduce its aggressiveness typically resolves this issue.

What is the Tongue Weight?

Your trailer's tongue weight is the load being supported by your tow vehicle. Just imagine physically lifting the front end of your trailer by the coupler. The weight you are supporting is the tongue weight. (Of course, this probably isn't possible unless you have superhuman strength, but you get the idea.) For a bumper pull horse trailer, the tongue weight is typically around 20% of the empty trailer's gross weight.

When calculating how much weight is on top of the trailer's tires, wheels, and axles, you must remove the tongue weight of the trailer. That's because a portion of that total weight will be transferred back to the tow vehicle, meaning it's carried completely by the tow vehicle and not by the trailer.

Remember our trailer weight example from earlier? If your trailer weighs 5,000 pounds and you haul three 1,200-pound horses, plus tack and gear, your total trailer weight will be **around 9,000 pounds**. If you had a 20% tongue weight, you'd have approximately 1,800 pounds of weight being carried by the tow vehicle. That means you'd have to subtract 1,800 pounds from the 9,000 pounds, meaning that your trailer's suspension is really only hauling around 7,200 pounds.

Side note: I typically perform the tongue weight calculation based on the trailer's empty weight, not loaded. The reason is most manufacturers position the trailer axles centered underneath where the horse stands, meaning when you load your horses most of their weight is directed over the axles. Your tongue weight will change some, but typically it's minimal. However, if you have the ability to load your horses and weigh your trailer to determine trailer weight, and tongue weight, then by all means that's the most accurate, and would be my preference.

To weigh a truck and trailer together on a scale and determine the trailer's tongue weight, you can follow these steps:

Step 1: Find a Public Weigh Station or Truck Scale

Look for a public weigh station, truck stop with a scale, or a commercial weighing service. Many truck stops, agricultural co-ops, and some local waste facilities have scales available for public use.

Step 2: Weigh the Truck and Trailer Together

- **Drive both the truck and trailer onto the scale** so that all axles are on the scale.

- **Record the total weight** displayed on the scale. This is the combined gross vehicle weight of the truck and trailer together.

Step 3: Weigh the Truck Alone

- **Detach the trailer** and set it aside. Ensure that the trailer jack is not on the scale.

- **Drive the truck back onto the scale** alone.

- **Record the weight** displayed on the scale. This is the weight of the truck alone (Truck GVW).

Step 4: Calculate the Trailer's Gross Weight

- **Subtract the truck's weight** from the combined

weight of the truck and trailer:

Step 5: Weigh the Truck with the Trailer's Tongue Weight Only

- **Reconnect the trailer** to the truck.

- **Position the truck on the scale** so that only the truck's axles (front and rear) are on the scale, but the trailer's axles are off the scale.

- **Record the weight** displayed on the scale. This weight includes the truck and the tongue weight of the trailer (Truck + Tongue Weight).

Step 6: Calculate the Trailer's Tongue Weight

- **Subtract the weight of the truck alone** from the weight of the truck with the tongue weight.

Example Calculation

- **Combined Weight (Truck + Trailer)**: 10,000 lbs.

- **Truck Weight (without trailer)**: 5,000 lbs.

- **Truck + Tongue Weight**: 6,000 lbs.

- **Trailer Gross Weight**: Trailer Gross Weight = 10,000 – 5,000 = 5,000 lbs.
- **Trailer Tongue Weight**: Tongue Weight = 6,000 – 5,000 = 1,000 lbs.

By following these steps, you can determine the trailer's gross weight and tongue weight, which are important for safe towing and ensuring that you do not exceed the vehicle's weight ratings.

Avoid Unnecessary Trailer Maintenance

When shopping for horse trailers, always remember: **just because something costs less money or more money doesn't mean it's necessarily better or worse**. Many manufacturers will use the cheapest axle and tires they can find, knowing that most trailer consumers only look at the overall features of the trailer. Most buyers assume the manufacturer installed a quality suspension system. But that's not always the case. The last thing you want is to be sitting on the side of the road with a blown-out tire or even worse, a damaged or broken axle. Maintenance on your trailer's suspension can be *very* expensive.

Tire Maintenance

When it comes to tire maintenance, we mentioned earlier that tires rarely *wear* out, but rather *age* out. Looking at the date code on the tire will give you an idea of its age. Then, you'll want to look at when the tire was put in service. That's the day you started using the trailer. Hauling your loaded trailer up and down the road causes heat to build up in the tire, along with the normal wear and tear from the exterior elements. So that's really the starting point for the age of the tire.

I recommend changing your tires every four or five years — regardless of the amount of tread on the tires. Sure, you may be able to get six or seven years of service out of them, but you're really running on borrowed time. To best preserve your tires, make sure you keep an eye on the air levels so that they're not over inflated or under inflated before each trip.

Hauling with under-inflated tires can cause excessive heat buildup. This can weaken the rubber compound and the sidewall of the tire. Though you may be able to haul several times like that, eventually it'll catch up with you and the tire will blow out.

There are many different tire pressure monitoring systems available. Putting tire pressure gauges on your horse trailer for each tire will help you know when to add air and help you tow much more safely.

One problem we often run across, particularly on new trailers, is making sure the trailer runs level with the tow vehicle. To fix this, we park the tow vehicle and the trailer on a flat surface and hook it up to the gooseneck. It's essential to measure the front and back corners of the trailer against the pavement, ensuring they're very close to equal. While a slight discrepancy of one to two inches between the front and back ends might not be catastrophic, it's crucial to adjust the trailer as close to level as possible.

To sum it all up, when it comes to tires and maintenance, change your tires at least every five years, make sure you keep the air up properly, and make sure your trailer is being towed level.

As long as you do those three things, nine times out of ten, you'll get really good service out of your tires. Oh, and avoid the curbs. Striking a curb during a turn or hitting something on the road will weaken or damage the sidewall of the tire and could lead to tire failure.

Bearing Maintenance

As for bearing maintenance, Dexter offers a **"Nev-R-Lube" axle system** that has excellent durability. It's basically a bearing running inside an oil bath and it lasts significantly longer than greased bearings.

They also offer what's called a **"Nev-R-Adjust" braking system**. Now, this doesn't mean the brakes will last for the next 20 years, but it does make repairs much easier. On a typical axle, as the pad wears the maintenance technician will need to pull the wheel, pull the hub, and tighten the springs to fix the portion of the pad that's worn. However, with a never-adjust braking system, that step can be skipped. Since the axle itself adjusts as the pad wears down, less maintenance is needed. The only thing you have to be aware of is changing the pads when they wear out.

Never-adjust braking systems and never-lube axle systems are more expensive, but they'll save you money on maintenance costs and headaches in the long run.

Axle Maintenance

Regarding axle suspension, check the maintenance record or the service schedule in the axle manufacturer manual or the owner's manual. The maintenance specifics depend on the manufacturer, the axle, the weight capacity, and the style of the axle. However, most will probably recommend inspecting every 12,000 miles.

The majority of folks rarely put 12,000 miles a year on a trailer, but mileage isn't the only factor you should consider. As your trailer sits in the elements — rain, moisture, extreme temperature, changing seasons — it will start to wear down. It's almost like your automobile. A lot of companies will recommend changing your oil, regardless of the mileage.

I recommend getting an annual inspection for your trailer at a qualified repair shop. A lot of folks reach out to us and ask questions about how to change a bearing or how to do the maintenance themselves. In my opinion, if you have to ask, you shouldn't be trying to do it yourself. You wouldn't call your local auto dealership and ask for instructions on how to change a part. (They would chuckle and ask you to schedule a service appointment.)

Take your trailer to someone who knows what they're doing, and spend the money on that annual inspection. At a qualified repair shop, they can easily pull the tire and the wheel, look at the braking system, and repack the bearings if needed. They'll make sure your trailer is ready to go. Remember, frequent trailer checkups prevent bigger, more serious, and more expensive maintenance problems later down the road.

Door Latches, Hinges, and Other Hardware: Functionality and Durability

When it comes to (horse) door latches and hinges, there are many things to consider including the door itself, how sturdy it is, and the type of latch that keeps the door shut. Remember, the trailer door and hinge is what secures your horse while traveling down the road at 60+ miles per hour.

Hinges need to be especially durable, since they must hold the door open and closed for 20 to 25 years. In most aluminum trailers, the back doors are secured using what's called a **strap hinge**. After using those in the past, I found they're more flimsy and not nearly as sturdy as other styles of hinges. The advantage to a strap hinge is that the hinge itself allows the door to fold around to the sidewall of the trailer. Often you can even latch the door against the trailer sidewall. Most hinges only fold at approximately 180 degrees, but strap hinges will fold closer to 270 degrees. There are pros and cons depending on which style of latch or hinge the trailer manufacturer used.

The majority of the (people) doors in your trailer — the entry door in the tack room or the dressing room door — are camper doors. There are several manufacturers of camper door latches, but they all accomplish the same purpose. Make sure you keep your camper door latches well lubricated. Just take the key, dip it in a jar of Vaseline, push and pull the key in and out of the lock a few times — and voila, now it's going to work 100% better. Lubrication is your friend! Do the same thing with the **striker plate** — the flat piece of metal with a hole that receives the spring-loaded latch to secure your door. Take the striker plate and spray some lube, WD-40, or another type of penetrating oil in those areas.

Don't forget about the strap hinge. To lubricate that, you can use penetrating oil (unless the hinge has a grease zerk, in which case a technician will need to grease it).

Broken door holdbacks are a common scenario that typically result from excessive pressure or force applied to the latch mechanism. While holdbacks are usually generic and can be replaced easily, it's essential to ensure they're used properly to prevent damage.

Another important (people) door is the exterior escape door in the horse stall. This door needs to be strong and sturdy. If a horse is standing in a front stall near the escape door, and begins to paw, weak doors will warp from the bottom. A horse could get a leg through by simply pushing the bottom of the door open.

You can test your door's strength using the broom test. Simply walk up to the door and open it, then try to close the door with a wooden broom handle shoved in the bottom corner. If the door warps or flexes at the top as you push on it really hard, or the bottom of the door cracks, the door itself is not built as strong as it should be.

Many manufacturers secure front stall escape doors with just a camper door lock — that's not nearly enough! Every single door inside the horse area should have double latches, especially on escape doors. These backup safety latches should be made from steel or powder coated steel, since those are going to be the strongest latches as well as the strongest hinges. A backup latch is a latch that's in addition to the standard so you will actually have two methods for securing the door. This way if one fails, the other is a backup. No matter what style of latch you decide on, make sure that they're installed well enough to hold a door closed — even with the weight of a 1,200+ pound horse kicking or pawing at the bottom of the door.

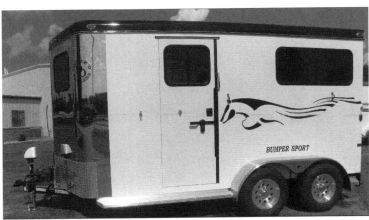

Photo showing an escape door with two latches. One primary, one back up.

Speaking of door hinges, I recently had a customer call and tell me that their back door hinge froze and broke the weld. It was a steel hinge with stainless steel on the inside and a grease fitting on top. The trailer was several years old and the grease fitting had never been touched. Don't expect door hinges to last forever — especially if you're not going to lubricate those. If you take the time to lubricate the hinges, they'll last the lifetime of the trailer. That's the purpose of lubrication.

With window latches, it's the same process. Make sure you lubricate, especially if it's a lockable window on a drop-down. As I mentioned earlier, lubricating a lock and key with Vaseline frees up a lock tremendously. You'll quickly notice how much easier that window will open and close.

Additionally, problems with drop-down or sliding windows often arise after trailers sit idle for extended periods of time. Lubricating these windows regularly helps prevent them from becoming stuck or difficult to open.

On a side note: a lot of windows will slide instead of swing open with a latch. Often — particularly when they're new — the inner rubber gasket can have a sticking effect that makes it difficult to open. Just spray some penetrating oil down in the track, in between the glass and the rubber piece, and that window will slide much better.

One more thing you should lubricate: the trailer ramp springs. Most ramps have springs that assist in lifting the ramp (taking some of that weight off of your back). These springs often are made of steel, and if you don't lubricate them, over time the ramp hinge and spring will start to seize up. If you can get penetrating oil for lubrication into those areas, it will make the ramp much easier to use. It also prevents the spring from breaking. If a spring isn't properly lubricated, it starts to bind, and then the spring itself will break. Fixing a broken spring is a time-consuming and costly maintenance issue.

In the long run, lack of maintenance is much more expensive than keeping a well-maintained trailer. Common wear and tear, if not taken care of, can cause big problems later on. Get your trailer checked yearly. If your trailer sits outdoors, invest in a trailer cover. Spending a few hundred dollars on a trailer cover or a yearly maintenance checkup will save you thousands over the years. And it'll keep your trailer looking new for a very long time.

Understanding Warranties and What They Cover

In my opinion, warranties are really a waste of time. Why? Because the majority of manufacturers write their warranties with a group of attorneys, assuring that it's almost entirely in *their* favor, not yours. And the majority of warranties advertised in the market today are very misleading.

I examined six of the top horse trailer manufacturers in the US. According to their websites, most advertise an eight or a ten-year structural warranty plus a one or two-year bumper-to-bumper warranty. The longest warranty I found was a ten-year structural warranty and a three-year bumper-to-bumper warranty. However, when I read the fine print, I discovered that structural warranty is on only a handful of components — the ones that will never fail on the trailer! If someone buys that trailer thinking they won't have to pay anything for ten years, they would surely be in for a rude awakening.

It's like your automobile manufacturer saying that they're going to give you a 20-year warranty on your vehicle — but it only covers the steel chassis or the frame that the vehicle is built on. That's not what breaks on your vehicle. It's all of the other components. The same thing happens with horse trailers, even with manufacturers that advertise a misleading bumper-to-bumper warranty. Often those warranties are only on the components they make in-house.

For example, if a builder makes their own door latches, they would warranty that door latch for up to three years. But they don't make the tires, the wheels, the axles, the wiring on the trailer, or many other components that are generally warrantied for only one year.

I always tell folks **warranties are only as good as the people that you're purchasing from.** If you're buying a new trailer through a dealer, make sure it's through a reputable one. That way, if you have problems that really shouldn't have happened, generally the dealer would take care of you because you're their customer (regardless of the warranty). But do make sure you read the fine print and fully understand what the warranty promises.

Brad's Trailer Tips & Takeaways:

- "The heavier the tires, the better" is a myth. Trailers are only as strong as the weakest link in the equation. Make sure your tires match your towing capacity and have at least a three-year warranty.

- Tires don't wear out, they age out. To keep your tires safe, keep them properly inflated and make sure you tow your trailer level. You should change your tires every four to five years, regardless of the amount of tread on the tires.

- Lubricate your trailer's door latches, hinges, locks, striker plates, and ramp springs with WD-40, Vaseline, or another lubricant to keep them in top condition.

- Most warranties are misleading; they're only as good as the person you're buying them from. Make sure to buy your trailer from a reputable dealer or manufacturer.

- If your trailer wheels are slinging grease, it means your braking system is set too tight. A quick adjustment can reduce breaking aggressiveness and quickly solve this common problem.

Chapter 5
Towing Safety & Vehicle Compatibility

Towing safety and vehicle compatibility is probably one of the most discussed topics trailer dealers and designers deal with during the building and sales process. It's also one of the most *misleading* things that vehicle manufacturers do (almost as misleading as trailer warranties). Clients reach out to us weekly with questions about this confusing topic. Let's look at an example:

"**My tow vehicle is rated to haul 14,000 pounds. I'm looking for a three-horse gooseneck trailer. The gooseneck weighs 5,000 pounds.**"

With horses, equipment, and tack, let's estimate that you'd need to haul around 10,000 pounds in this scenario. The tow vehicle is rated for 14,000 pounds. Common sense would tell you that if you have 4,000 or 5,000 pounds of extra capacity from the tow vehicle, your vehicle would easily handle hauling that trailer. But that's **not the case**.

There are a lot of terms or terminology that get really confusing, and quite honestly, it makes my head hurt. I'm not sure why they try to complicate things so much. I don't understand why vehicle manufacturers always advertise the largest number or capacity that the tow vehicle is capable of, without ever focusing on the fine print. **Remember, a load is only as strong as the weakest link**.

So if a vehicle is "capable" of towing 14,000 pounds but it'll only carry 2,000 pounds, *then you really just have a vehicle that's rated to carry 2,000 pounds*. I know that statement is a little confusing, so let's dive into the specifics...

There are a few common terms you'll probably run across during your research process for tow vehicles and trailers. I will address the specifics of both. The first is **GVWR**, or Gross Vehicle Weight Rating. This has nothing to do with the weight of the vehicle or the trailer. Every trailer manufactured in the United States has the GVWR stamped right on the VIN Plate and many people think that's the weight of the trailer, but that's *incorrect*.

Very few manufacturers, if any, actually stamp the *weight of the trailer* on the VIN Plate.

For horse trailers, GVWR simply means the **capacity of the tires, wheels, and axles**. In my opinion, when it comes to trailers, you don't really need to worry about it. In the end, it's up to the manufacturer to decide and make sure that the suspension is properly rated to the load being carried. So as a consumer, the GVWR of a trailer in relation to your tow vehicle is much less important than the payload of a vehicle, which we will discuss in a moment. For tow vehicles, GVWR again is the capacity of the tires, wheels, and axles. Basically, how much the drive, suspension system, and chassis can handle. This would include the weight of the vehicle along with passengers, cargo, trailer tongue weight, etc.

Another fancy term in horse trailers is **GAWR**, which stands for Gross Axle Weight Rating. This is the maximum amount of weight your trailer's axles can support. If you have a 7,000 pound suspension, for example, the GVWR is 7,000 pounds. The GAWR is 3,500 pounds per axle, at least on the trailer.

For tow vehicles, GAWR stands for the same thing. Again, another term that in my opinion really doesn't matter in the towing equation. It is important, but truly all we are looking for is what a vehicle can pull, and what it can carry. Once that is determined, GAWR and GVWR are irrelevant terms to focus on. Example: Chevy isn't going to rate a vehicle to carry 2,000 pounds of load in the bed, but yet it would exceed the back axle rating (GAWR). The axle is going to have enough capacity to support the 2,000 pounds Chevy says it can handle.

The last term that you'll see often is **GVW**, or Gross Vehicle Weight. That's simply the empty weight of the trailer, or the empty weight of a tow vehicle. Example, if a horse trailer weight is 3,500 pounds that means the GVW is 3,500 pounds. If an empty tow vehicle weighs 4,000 pounds, that means the GVW (often referred to as curb weight) is 4,000 pounds. As a trailer designer, when it's time for us to sell a trailer and determine if a client's tow vehicle is sufficient, the only thing that we are looking for is the overall weight of the empty trailer, trailer's tongue weight, along with the weight of the cargo being hauled — the horses, the tack, and the gear.

What a tow vehicle is capable of *carrying* is NOT the same as what it can *tow*.

Just think of trying to move a heavy piece of furniture in your home, such as a dresser or a couch. You can probably slide it around on the floor — which is what you could tow or pull. But if you have to pick up one end of it and drag it around, that would make it heavier — that's the payload, or what you can carry. Tow vehicles are the same way, but manufacturers *rarely* advertise what the vehicle can actually carry, which is also called the "payload."

Luckily, you can easily calculate the payload with the right information. Remember, payload is simply how much the vehicle can carry. To calculate this, you take the vehicle's GVWR and subtract the empty weight of the vehicle (GVW). That difference is your available payload which is what your vehicle can "carry." Formula for vehicle payload calculation: GVWR of tow vehicle - curb weight of tow vehicle (GVW) = payload, or how much weight your vehicle can *really* carry.

For example, if a tow vehicle has 7,000 pound GVWR and the tow vehicle weighs 5,000 pounds (which is the GVW, or curb weight) then you have 2,000 pounds remaining capacity which is called payload. In order to not exceed the tow vehicle's payload, you need to add up the weight of yourself as a driver, weight of any passengers, weight of any cargo, and weight of the trailer's tongue weight. It doesn't matter if it's a bumper pull, or a gooseneck, or a pickup truck or SUV, the calculation to determine if you are exceeding payload capacity will be the same.

People will often make the mistake of looking at the manufacturer's really large number, bragging that's what their vehicle will tow. When they read the fine print and try to calculate the payload of the vehicle, it's much less impressive.

For example, a Chevy Tahoe or Chevy Suburban has a tow capacity of around 8,000 pounds. Most folks think, "Well, if I purchase a trailer that weighs 4,000 pounds, and put two horses in it at 1,000 pounds each . . . I'm carrying 6,000 pounds. My vehicle will pull 8,000 pounds, so I'm in the safe zone, no problem!"

The problem with this thought process is that it doesn't take into account the **trailer's tongue weight**. What the vehicle actually pulls is different than how much of the trailer weight is pressing down on the back hitch of your tow vehicle, also known as tongue weight.

Most bumper pulls have about a 20% tongue weight. So a 4,000-pound empty trailer would have approximately an 800-pound tongue weight. A Chevy Tahoe today has about an 800-pound tongue weight rating — and that's using a weight distribution system.

That means . . . you do not have as much cushion in the safe zone as you thought, and you need weight distribution.

What is weight distribution?

Weight distribution systems simply take the weight of the trailer that presses down on the back of the tow vehicle and distributes a portion of the weight back to the front end of the tow vehicle. This allows the tires and the front suspension to plant firmly on the ground, which results in better vehicle control, especially if you have to swerve quickly to avoid hitting something.

When it comes to gooseneck trailers, we face the same challenges with vehicle capacity and trailer tongue weight. I hate to say anything brand specific, but in my years of experience, Dodge tow vehicles typically have the *lowest* payload rating when compared to GMC, Chevy, or Ford vehicles.

A lot of clients will come to us with a half-ton or a three-quarter-ton Dodge with a really large towing capacity (14,000 plus pounds), but when you calculate the payload, it may be 2,000 pounds or less. To put that in perspective, for most goosenecks, an average percentage of tongue weight would be around 30% of the trailer's overall empty weight. For example, if a gooseneck weighs 8,000 pounds, then you could estimate the tongue weight to be around 2,400 pounds. So if you have a tow vehicle that has a payload of only 2,000 pounds, you will exceed the manufacturer's stated tow rating for that vehicle.

To sum it all up, there are really only three numbers to focus on when trying to determine the safety and adequacy of a tow vehicle:

#1 Total Trailer Weight

This is the overall weight of the trailer (including your tack, gear, and horses). Again, if you're hauling 10,000 pounds worth of load, make sure that the tow vehicle is rated to pull or tow a minimum of 10,000 pounds.

You must know the overall weight you're hauling to make sure your vehicle will **pull it**.

#2 Trailer Tongue Weight

Unfortunately, this information is often difficult to obtain because manufacturers don't list it. In fact, a lot of manufacturers and dealers probably don't even know it — they just estimate or worse, tell unsuspecting buyers what they want to hear just to make the sale.

The only true way to calculate tongue weight is to have the trailer weighed **and** the tongue weight of the trailer weighed. That may not always be practical, but if you purchase a vehicle or a trailer and you want to ensure your load is safe, it's absolutely necessary. You can weigh your trailer at a scale, like a big truck stop or an 18-wheeler area. There you can find the loaded weight of the trailer as well as the trailer's tongue weight. If purchasing from a dealer, insist the dealer provide a certified weigh station certificate so that you know the weight up front.

#3 Payload

To calculate the payload, which determines the vehicle portion, subtract the vehicle's weight from the vehicle's GVWR. This will tell you how much weight you can carry. This number must be bigger than your trailer's tongue weight. Vehicle weight you would look up in the vehicle manufacturer specs, or contact the vehicle manufacturer with your VIN and they can provide the information.

You must know the trailer's tongue weight and your tow vehicle's payload to make sure your vehicle will **carry it**. **Don't just take the dealer's word for it . . . unfortunately many sales folks will "fudge" to make a sale.**

Make sure the payload of the vehicle will carry the tongue weight of the trailer, and the tow rating of the vehicle will pull the overall weight. As long as those parameters are met, you're in the safe zone with any type of load.

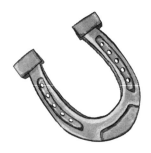

Brad's Trailer Tips & Takeaways:

- What a vehicle is capable of carrying is NOT the same as what it can pull. The payload is what your trailer is actually capable of carrying.

- For towing safety, make sure the payload of the vehicle will carry the tongue weight of the trailer, and the tow rating of the vehicle will pull the overall weight.

- When trying to determine the safety and adequacy of a tow vehicle, there are three numbers to know: (1) total trailer weight, (2) trailer tongue weight, and (3) the payload.

- Make sure your trailer runs level with your tow vehicle — even just a slight imbalance can cause dangerous road accidents and costly repairs.

Chapter 6
Safety First

Essential Safety Features in Horse Trailers

When shopping for a new horse trailer, it's easy to get swept away by beautiful marketing and shiny new paint jobs. However, there are some very practical safety features your trailer should *absolutely* have before you make your purchase.

Multiple Horse Exits:

It's important to have different exit points in the trailer. A side ramp, in addition to the rear door, helps you quickly and safely unload your horses during an emergency situation. It also gives you better access to individual horses so you can quickly give attention to one in distress. This setup is a standard safety feature I recommend for all horse trailers.

Brakes and Lighting:

A well-functioning braking system and adequate external and internal lighting are non-negotiable for safety. These features ensure you're prepared for travel during any time of the day and under varying weather conditions.

Ventilation:

Proper airflow is crucial. Functional windows and, if possible, additional ventilation systems like built-in fans make all the difference. This keeps the air fresh and helps keep the trailer at a comfortable temperature. Remember, a hot trailer means a hot horse — one who is going to sweat excessively and become dehydrated.

Interior Lighting:

Good lighting inside the trailer can significantly reduce stress for horses, especially during loading and unloading. It makes the trailer much more inviting and less intimidating, encouraging the horses to enter and exit without fuss.

Flooring:

Comfort underfoot is critical for the horses' well-being during transport. I prefer using high-quality materials like Rumber for flooring because it's durable, easy to maintain, and provides good traction.

Safety Gear for Towing:

Never overlook the importance of safety chains, cables, and an emergency breakaway system. These are vital for preventing the trailer from separating from the tow vehicle if an unexpected disconnect occurs.

Feed and Water Supplies:

Long trips mean you need to have adequate arrangements for feeding and watering the horses. Make sure there are enough hay nets, feed bags, and water containers accessible during the journey to keep your horses hydrated and fed.

Horse Trailer Camera (Bonus!):

Horse trailer cameras are certainly not a necessary safety feature, but I highly recommend installing one in your trailer. It's the best way to keep a constant eye on your horses during travel. A lot can happen while in transit and being able to check on your horses whenever you want provides invaluable peace of mind.

Essential First Aid Supplies

Traveling with your horses is both an exciting adventure and a serious responsibility. Ensuring you're prepared for any medical emergencies by carrying a comprehensive horse first aid kit in your trailer is essential for the safety and comfort of your equine companions.

A thorough first aid kit allows you to address minor injuries on the spot and stabilize more serious conditions until professional help is available. It is crucial to be well-prepared to efficiently handle any unexpected situations while on the road.

Kit Preparation and Storage:

Your first aid kit should be easy to access and meticulously organized. Consider storing it in a compact, segmented container like a tackle box or a robust tool box that's both water-resistant and airtight to keep the contents clean and dry. Placing the kit in an easily accessible area, such as the front of your trailer or a designated compartment, ensures you can access it quickly in emergencies.

Contents of the Kit:

The kit should include basic veterinary tools and supplies such as a stethoscope, thermometer (with Vaseline for lubrication), and a variety of bandages and wound care products. Essentials like flashlights, scissors, duct tape, and gloves are also important. Make sure you have all necessary items for treating wounds, administering medication, and potentially sedating your horse if needed.

Medications and Treatments:

Include a range of medications as recommended by your veterinarian — pain relievers (e.g., Phenylbutazone or Banamine), sedatives, and electrolyte pastes. Have materials ready for wound cleaning and dressing, like antiseptic scrubs (Betadine), hydrogen peroxide, and gauze. Items for specific treatments — such as Epsom salts for infection drawing and fly spray — should also be included.

Regular Checks and Updates:

It's vital to routinely check your first aid kit, ideally on a monthly basis. Replace used or expired items immediately to maintain readiness. Keeping your vet's contact information in the kit and knowing basic horse vital signs and how to check them can save your horse's life in an emergency situation.

Travel-Specific Considerations:

Since space may be limited during travel, your safety kit should be tailored to include only essential items that might be needed urgently. In these situations, immediate response is crucial. However, having a more extensive first aid station setup at your home base is advisable for comprehensive care.

Personal Preparedness:

Familiarize yourself with the first aid procedures. Knowing what to do and how to use the items in your kit can significantly improve the outcome for your horse in an emergency. A quick review of a first aid guide before trips can be very beneficial.

Essential Resources and Contacts

For horse owners, having a solid list of essential resources and contacts is crucial for ensuring the well-being and safety of their horses. Here are some contacts and resources that I believe should be on every horse owner's radar.

- Veterinary Care Providers (This includes local vets and emergency vet services.)
- Farriers

- Feed and Supply Stores

- Equine Transport Services

- Equine Insurance Agents

- Local Equine Associations

- Online Resources (*American Association of Equine Practitioners* is a great resource for finding up-to-date horse care practices.)

- Local Horse Community Contacts

Having these resources organized and easily accessible can improve the efficiency of managing emergencies and the general care of your horses. It's not just about having the numbers; it's about building a network of trusted professionals and fellow enthusiasts who support each other in responsible horse ownership. Always make sure to review and update your contacts list regularly, ensuring that all information is current.

Brad's Trailer Tips & Takeaways:

- Safety is the most important feature in your horse trailer! Make sure your trailer is built with quality materials that protect your horse from danger, maintain a cool and comfortable temperature in the trailer, and provide a smooth and enjoyable ride, every time.

- Your trailer should have the following essential safety features: multiple exits, well-functioning brakes, vehicle lighting, proper ventilation, interior lighting, adequate flooring, safety gear for towing, feed, water, and first-aid supplies, and a horse trailer camera.

- Create a thorough list of essential resources and contacts to have on hand in your trailer in case of an emergency and remember to update it regularly.

Chapter 7
Horse Comfort & Welfare

Loading and Unloading Techniques to Minimize Stress and Risk of Injury

The storm clouds were rolling in over the showgrounds when a woman named Kathy desperately tried to load her quarter horse mare onto the back of a four-horse straight load trailer. She tried food. She tried pulling. She tried getting a friend to tap the horse from the back. Then she tried probably six other methods you've likely read about in articles. Nothing worked.

The wind was kicking up and fat raindrops were starting to fall as the mare stood there, legs planted, nostrils flat, and ears pointed to the back. She was not getting on that trailer. Finally, two men came up behind Kathy's horse and linked their arms behind the pony's rump.

They pushed . . . Kathy pulled . . . and the surprised mare finally stumbled onto the trailer right before the storm started to take hold.

I hear stories like this all the time. It's not uncommon to see horses hesitating or outright refusing to board trailers. This could be for many reasons — anything from bad past experiences to simply the fear of the unknown. Since horses are prey animals, they are wired to be wary of potential traps and confinements, and as a result, many resist loading.

When it comes to loading and unloading horses from trailers, it's all about minimizing stress and reducing the risk of injury. Through years of experience, I've honed a few techniques that seem to work best for keeping both horses and handlers safe. Here are my best practices.

Loading Techniques

#1. Be Prepared

Make sure your horse is familiar with the trailer. Practice loading and unloading frequently, even when you don't have a trip planned. Show them the trailer is not dangerous by encouraging them to come near it using treats.

#2. Stay Calm

If you can, before loading, spend some quality time with your horse. This can calm any nerves they might be having, and reassure them that everything is going to be okay. A calm horse is a horse that's much easier to load.

#3. Check Your Environment

Just like it's important for your horse to be calm, it's also important for your loading environment to be calm, as well. Now, this is not always possible. Sometimes you need to load a horse at a loud and busy show. That being said, whenever possible, try to keep the environment around the trailer quiet and free of any disturbances that could spook your horse.

#4. Follow the Leader

Horses pick up on our emotions, so make sure you are calm and relaxed as well. If you're nervous about loading, your horse will sense it. Walk confidently into your horse trailer and encourage your horse to follow. I've also found that it can be helpful when loading multiple horses, to **load your better loader first**. This allows your other horses to observe and then follow the leader.

#5. Use Rewards

Rewards are controversial for some folks, but if it works, it works. Have some treats to hand to reward your horse once they have loaded into the trailer. Positive reinforcement training can be really helpful for a lot of horses. These can of course be used for unloading, too.

Unloading Techniques

#1. Be Patient

Patience is key! Some horses are ready to run out of the trailer as soon as the door opens. Some horses are more hesitant. Take your time. Rushing could startle your horse and lead to injuries — for your horses or for you.

#2. Guide, Don't Pull

Avoid pulling or forcing your horse out. Encourage your horses by guiding them with a lead rope.

#3. Be Consistent

Horses love predictability. Try to keep your unloading routine consistent.

#4. Proceed with Caution

Once you're at your destination, I always suggest doing a quick inspection before unloading your horses. Make sure that nothing has shifted during travel that could injure or spook your horse while unloading.

Trailer Modifications for Easier Loading and Unloading

If you have an anxious horse that doesn't like to load in the trailer, you know just how difficult it can be to coax them in and out of the trailer. While training techniques do help, the design, comfort, and build of your trailer can also make things easier. Here are a few essential trailer features that make loading painless for both anxious horses and easy loaders.

Ramps Instead of Step-Ups: While this is a somewhat controversial topic, after loading many different horses in different trailers over the years, I've found that ramps often result in a much less complicated loading and unloading process. Horses seem to find ramps less intimidating than a step-up design. The not-so-steep steep incline makes getting in and out of the trailer much easier for them.

Side Load Options with Wide Doors: Incorporating an extra wide side door and a ramp can be a helpful feature for easier loading and unloading. This horse trailer design allows the horse to walk straight through the trailer, without ever having to back out. Making a horse back out is against their natural instincts and tends to make loading more stressful than it needs to be. The straight walk-through setup is less likely to cause a horse to panic.

Customizable Stalls: I always recommend customizing stalls to fit your horses. This gives them the appropriate amount of space. You can also determine your horse's preferred orientation — whether they prefer forward-facing or reverse-facing — which can greatly reduce trailer anxiety.

Brad's Trailer Tips & Takeaways:

- If your horse is a difficult loader, try loading through a ramp on the side door. This allows your horse to walk into the stall (in a backwards facing configuration) and walk out the back door to unload after arriving at your destination.

- Customizable stalls that fit your horse's size perfectly can reduce trailer anxiety tremendously. Make sure your trailer is open, clean, well-lit, and well-ventilated so your horse can be comfortable and calm during travel.

Chapter 8
Trailer Maintenance & Upkeep

Even though maintenance and upkeep are crucial for your horse trailer's longevity, they are very often overlooked or forgotten. Regardless of the material or manufacturer, regular maintenance is key to ensuring the trailer's durability.

Regular Maintenance Checks

As mentioned previously, one of the best preventive measures is to either store the trailer indoors or use a trailer cover, which could cost a few hundred dollars. This helps protect the trailer from elements such as rain, snow, extreme temperatures, and especially sunlight — which can severely deteriorate paint finishes, rubber gaskets, and other components.

Many owners find it cumbersome to cover their trailers regularly. A client of mine devised a simple solution by attaching sandbags to one side of the cover, making it easier to deploy by just tossing the sandbags over the trailer. This method effectively keeps the cover in place and simplifies the process.

Regular checks — such as monitoring tire pressure and inspecting door hinges, latches, and windows — are essential before any trip. These checks are crucial because trailer tires often lose pressure over time. Making sure they are fully inflated before travel can significantly improve performance when hauling.

If you don't travel frequently with your trailer, annual maintenance is usually sufficient. This should include lubricating door locks (by dipping a key in Vaseline and using it on the locks), and applying penetrating oil on striker plates, door latches, window hinges, and other movable parts. If your trailer has greasable hinges, using a grease gun to lubricate them at least once a year is a great idea. Other components, like the rear ramp latches and springs, also require regular lubrication to function smoothly.

Although these tasks are seemingly manageable, many trailer owners might not have the necessary tools or knowledge for proper maintenance. That's why it's important to take your trailer to a professional service annually for a comprehensive checkup.

The professionals will typically grease the locks, check the wheel bearings, inspect the overall structural integrity, and of course, examine the emergency breakaway system. This system is not only essential for safety; it's also required by federal law to function properly in case of an incident. Additionally, it's advisable to replace the battery in the emergency system every year, since this component is often overlooked (a repair shop can also do this for you at your annual inspection).

Over time, the rubber components and seals in trailers can degrade, especially if exposed to harsh environmental conditions. This degradation can lead to leaks and other issues that might not be immediately apparent, but cause significant problems down the line. That's why you must check these components as part of your regular maintenance routine.

When preparing for trips, it's crucial to always have a trailer jack and a spare tire ready. It's also a good idea to bring a small jack block with you — especially if your trailer has dual tires on each side. If the front tire is flat, you can back the trailer onto the block with the rear tire, lifting the front off the ground for easy replacement. Conversely, if the rear tire is flat, driving the front tire onto the block will elevate the rear tire off the ground. This method simplifies the tire change process significantly, making it a handy trick for any trailer owner to remember.

While it might be tempting to save money by handling maintenance yourself, these important tasks can be complex. Forgetting something or doing something wrong could cost you in the long run. That's why it's best to leave it to the professionals.

Cleaning Your Trailer

Regular cleaning of your horse trailer is also essential. It not only preserves the appearance but also prevents costly repairs down the line. During a detailed cleaning, you can spot small issues that need fixing — before they turn into major problems. It's also part of keeping your trailer safe for your horses, ensuring they aren't injured by any sharp edges or objects that could harm them during transit.

Here's a simple breakdown to guide you through the process if you're not sure where to start:

Exterior Cleaning: Begin with the exterior of your trailer. Use automotive soap and water to wash the body of the trailer. Pay special attention to the tires, corners, and undercarriage. Washing from top to bottom ensures that dirt from the roof doesn't streak down the sides you've just cleaned.

Living Quarters: If your trailer has living quarters, treat it like you would your home. Regular household cleaners work fine here. Don't forget to clean and maintain appliances and fixtures, as these can harbor mold and bacteria if left unused for too long.

Trailer Floors: This is crucial, as the condition of the floors can directly affect your horse's safety. Avoid materials like aluminum for flooring as it can corrode quickly if not properly cleaned, plus it has a high heat transfer rate.

Instead, opt for stronger materials like Rumber or quality wood, which are durable and easier to maintain as well as cooler. If cleaning a Rumber floor, simply hose off and allow it to dry. No rubber mat is needed. If you have a wood floor, remove the rubber mats after each use, hose down, and allow the floor to dry completely before installing the mats. This will keep your floor in good shape for the life of the trailer.

If you are working with an aluminum floor, that's okay, just make sure you remove the mats after each use and hose the floor well. Allow it to dry before installing the mats. Horse urine can cause aluminum floors to oxidize so it's important to keep your floor clean.

Don't Miss These Areas:

- **Roof and Window Sills:** Regularly check and clean the roof to prevent leakage.

- **Hinges and Keyholes:** Keep these areas lubricated and clean to ensure they function smoothly.

- **Trailer Padding:** Check for tears or breaks in the padding that could harm your horse and repair them promptly.

Rust Prevention and Cleaning: Regular checks for rust, especially in critical structural areas, are necessary. Use rust-resistant paints and primers to cover and protect any areas that show signs of rust.

Seasonal Maintenance: It's important to thoroughly clean and inspect your trailer at least twice a year. Use this opportunity to check everything — from the integrity of the floors and walls to the functionality of the brakes and lights.

Keep in mind that maintaining a trailer isn't just about aesthetics; it's about safety and longevity.

Storing and Securing Your Trailer

When it comes to trailer security and storage, the best way to protect your trailer is by keeping it indoors where it can be locked up, protecting it from both the elements and theft. However, many owners must resort to outdoor storage at a barn or a similar location. Many times this area is often shared with others, which can unfortunately increase the risk of theft.

Spare tires, batteries, tack, and gear are some of the most commonly stolen items. Despite the potential for security systems, practical and effective solutions are limited.

For those storing a trailer outdoors, simple security measures like using a high-quality lock on the coupler of the trailer and the trailer wheels can deter thieves. These locks should be robust enough to resist bolt cutters. However, these precautions are merely deterrents. A determined thief can overcome them, but might instead move on to an easier target if your trailer appears well-secured.

Maintaining Your Trailer Battery

If your trailer has an auxiliary battery (one that looks like a car battery), you need to ensure it's fully charged. Particularly if your trailer has a hydraulic jack or an electric jack. Almost on a weekly basis we receive a complaint from a client that their jack doesn't work, or either their interior horse lights aren't functioning. More often than not it's a weak or dead battery on the trailer.

Just this week I had a client contact me that his hydraulic jack wouldn't function, and inside trailer lights would not work. He said he "plugged" in the trailer to the truck but it didn't help. Short version of the story, his vehicle didn't have an active auxiliary circuit for charging the trailer battery while in transit, and the trailer battery was completely dead.

Most folks think, "oh I can just hook up my tow vehicle and that will take care of it." Unfortunately, that's incorrect. Sure your tow vehicle will help **maintain** your charged battery while in transit, but if you hook up and are ready to roll to a show with a dead trailer battery, the wiring on the tow vehicle is too small to carry enough amps to fully recharge the trailer battery properly.

For this reason, I recommend using a battery tender when the trailer is not in use. This means purchasing a battery charger that you would leave connected at all times while the trailer is parked at your home or barn. It will require a 110V plug in but if you keep it charged, it will prolong the life of the battery significantly and more important your trailer battery is ready to roll at all times.

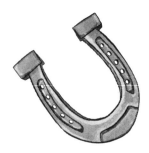

Brad's Trailer Tips & Takeaways:

- To keep your horse trailer working properly, take it to a professional for a comprehensive checkup every year, keep it covered to protect it from the elements, and regularly clean both the interior and exterior.

- If you store your trailer in a shared space, using a strong, robust, high-quality lock on the coupler of the trailer and the trailer wheels can deter thieves.

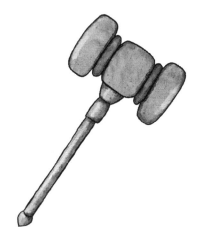

Chapter 9
Legal & Compliance

When it comes to legal compliance, most of the responsibility falls on the trailer manufacturer. Agencies like the National Highway Traffic and Safety Administration oversee manufacturing and set guidelines for trailer manufacturers. However, there are very few regulations specific to horse trailers concerning crash testing or the materials used.

As a manufacturer, I've noticed that there is not a rigorous check by government entities to ensure trailers meet specific safety or impact standards. For that reason, many trailers have unsafe designs or features that could cause problems for horses and their owners. That's why it's so important to choose a reputable trailer brand known for its safety standards. It's also a good idea to look up any historical accident information about the brand to understand how well their trailers withstand accidents.

Federal regulations dictate necessary safety features such as the number and type of brakes on the axles, the placement and color of lights, the emergency breakaway system, and the use of chains or cables for emergency purposes. The North American Trailer Dealers Association (NATDA) provides compliance certifications to manufacturers who meet these criteria, and it's advisable to purchase from dealers who offer trailers with the NATDA sticker, ensuring compliance with US laws.

Key Federal Requirements for Horse Trailer Owners

While the constructional integrity of the trailer is up to the trailer manufacturers, there are some important legal requirements for horse owners. Make sure you have the following information up to date and at hand before planning to travel with your horse trailer.

1. **Registration and Inspection**

    - All trailers must be properly registered and frequently inspected as per state and federal guidelines. This includes periodic DOT inspections to ensure safety standards are met.

2. **Vehicle Identification Number (VIN)**
   - Your trailer must have a VIN that complies with federal regulations, helping in its identification and compliance checks.

3. **Legal Load Limits**
   - It's crucial to know your total weight and comply with it in order to avoid penalties and ensure safety on the roads.

4. **Animal Welfare Laws**
   - Federal and state laws also regulate the transportation of animals, ensuring your horses travel in safe, humane conditions.

5. **Driving Licenses and Electronic Logging Devices (ELD)**
   - Depending on the weight of your trailer and your usage (commercial vs. non-commercial), you might need a Commercial Driver's License (CDL) and possibly an ELD.

The responsibility of the trailer owner primarily involves ensuring the trailer is insured and meets liability standards. Trailer insurance can often be bundled with your vehicle insurance, though terms can vary significantly by provider. It's essential to verify that your insurance covers not only liability but also physical damage to the trailer to protect against various risks, including accidents and natural disasters. Discussing all potential scenarios with your insurance agent beforehand can prevent unpleasant surprises in the event of an incident.

Brad's Trailer Tips & Takeaways:

- The structural integrity and manufacturing requirements to make your trailer legal for the road are the trailer manufacturer's responsibility. When buying a new trailer, choose a reputable trailer brand to ensure your trailer is safe and fit for the road.

- Every trailer owner should register their vehicle according to state and federal guidelines, have a vehicle identification number, tow within legal load limits, abide by animal welfare laws, and of course, have a valid driver's license.

- Make sure your insurance covers not only liability but also physical damage to the trailer (protecting you against both traffic accidents and natural disasters).

Chapter 10
Buying Guide

Getting Started

Purchasing a horse trailer can often feel overwhelming due to the wide range of opinions and options available. It's essential to set a *realistic budget*, while also understanding that focusing too strictly on cost can be limiting. Many clients have a specific number in mind, and attempt to fit all their desired features within this budget. However, this can lead to compromises on quality or features.

Approach horse trailers as a "want" rather than a "need." Unlike basic necessities like transportation or housing, a horse trailer is a *luxury* that enables you to engage in your passion for riding. Therefore, it should meet all your requirements to ensure maximum satisfaction. Often, clients set initial budgets without thorough research and end up either overspending or feeling dissatisfied with their purchase because they didn't initially invest in the trailer that truly met their needs.

When considering what to look for in a trailer, it's important to define your needs clearly:

- **Number of Horses:** Determine how many horses you need to transport regularly to avoid paying for unneeded capacity or finding yourself with too little space.

- **Trailer Configuration:** Decide whether you need a slant load or straight load — which will affect the trailer's internal layout and the ease of loading and unloading your horses.

- **Tow Vehicle:** Make sure your vehicle is capable of safely towing the trailer. This includes verifying the vehicle's towing capacity and payload to ensure it can safely handle the trailer's weight and tongue weight.

Practical considerations like these are fundamental to making an informed purchase. Additionally, consider long-term satisfaction over short-term savings. Opting for a trailer that truly fits your needs might cost more upfront, but it can prevent future disappointment and additional expenditure.

Remember, **a trailer's true cost is the difference in what you pay for it versus what you can sell it for.** Since the COVID-19 pandemic and the rising rate of inflation, we've had a number of clients use their trailers for only a few years, then sell it for as much (and sometimes more) than they originally paid. In this case, their true trailer cost was zero.

When it comes to negotiation, focus on *getting the right features at a fair price*, rather than simply seeking the lowest possible cost. Ensuring the trailer meets your specific needs is more important than getting a small discount. Always strive to work with reputable dealers who provide transparent pricing and quality service.

Other buying tips to keep in mind:

Research is key. Spend time understanding different horse trailer types and their specific features. This will help you in making an educated decision that aligns with your needs.

Future-proofing. Consider how your needs might evolve. You may only have one horse now, but will you purchase more in the future? You may not go on longer trips now, but you might one day. Think of all of the possibilities to ensure your horse trailer is a lifelong investment.

Buying a trailer isn't just a transaction; it's about making an informed decision that affects your and your horses' safety and comfort.

The Right Horse Trailer Makes ALL the Difference

Over the years, I've had the opportunity to talk with hundreds, if not thousands, of horse owners. Their experiences with horse trailers have ranged from average, to great, to downright horrendous!

Many folks realize, only after buying a new, safer trailer, just how uncomfortable or dangerous their old trailer was — and just how big of a difference the right horse trailer can make. It's no understatement to say that for many horse owners, the difference is like night and day.

THREE TRAILERS IN THREE YEARS

That was the case for Jamethiel M, a horse owner from Oregon. She started off her horse trailering experience with an old, two-horse, straight load trailer — which she hated!

She says: "My best friend, with amazing generosity, gifted me her a tiny little black trailer — but boy did my old gelding and I hate it! I refused to haul him in it more than a handful of times because every time, we both felt awful and stressed.

"I eventually sold it to a lady who planned to turn it into a mobile sauna for rafters and skiers — a much better fate, in my opinion, than asking another horse to travel in it. With those funds another friend gave me a screaming deal on a nice little Morgan Built two-horse stock trailer.

"But my horse, Tarma, clearly didn't love the trailer. She would load onto the trailer, eventually, but every adventure started out with a stressful load and haul.

"During one trip with friends, Tarma loaded onto my friend's trailer without any hesitation. I was shocked. No fuss, no whining, she just walked right in. Perhaps that's due to being hauled with a friend, maybe it's because of the trailer itself.

"My friend has a Double D Trailer. I've been drooling over it for years, and clearly, Tarma much prefers it. For loading, it makes a huge difference. It has a side load option with a larger front stall, and reverse facing hauling with ramps. The horses never have to turn around to load. It's much more comfortable for Tarma.

"So I decided to get my own. In the span of three years of actually owning horses I've gone from a tiny little black trailer that both my horse and I hated, to a nice little Morgan Built stock-sided trailer, to a custom-built Double D, which I refer to as the BMW's of horse trailers.

"I couldn't love my new trailer more, and I highly recommend Double D Trailers as the BMW of trailers. Their build quality, features, and ability to customize every inch of your trailer is unmatched.

"The main features and reason I went with Double D Trailers over Trails West or Featherlite include: side load, reverse facing, ramps, swing out SafeTack©, standard walk-thru door, standard insulation of dressing room and horse area, Rumber flooring, and the extra-large dressing room — among many others.

"My mare, Tarma, who isn't the most comfortable hauler, will self-load on this trailer — something she's not done on the five other trailers I've asked her to haul in.

"I can tell she's so much more comfortable through the cameras. She no longer dances around when big rigs or motorcycles pass us. She more or less self-loads now without complaint (though she does get testy when her gelding friend isn't loaded as fast as she'd like).

"Tarma has spent around 150 hours hauling in it for trips and day hauls, both solo and with a friend's horse. Her longest haul was 6 hours straight, up and home from the Cross State Ride. It is absurdly easy to feed her beet pulp mash at road stops through the drop down windows, and adjusting the temperature in the trailer is doable with all the windows, vents and fans.

"I love my trailer. I adore having it parked in front of my house, so I can tinker with it endlessly. Most of all, I love the freedom and comfort it brings. Every trip starts much more relaxed and the trailer tows smooth as glass."

The Dangers of Aluminum Horse Trailers

Research is key to making an educated decision and finding the right horse trailer. After reading this comprehensive guide, you'll be much more prepared when looking at trailers and you'll know exactly what you want (and what you don't want).

This makes the trailer buying process much easier, and ensures you'll be happy with the trailer you choose. That's what happened to Mike, a firefighter from South Carolina. When he realized the dangers of aluminum horse trailers, he knew that was not the type of trailer he wanted.

He says: "As a firefighter, I had an opportunity to attend a three-day large animal rescue class. After seeing what an accident can do to an aluminum trailer, we thought it might be a good time to look at getting rid of our aluminum trailer.

"We started an extensive internet search, and all paths led us to Double D Trailers. We ordered a 2 Horse SafeTack© Reverse Living Quarters Trailer. We were very impressed with the thought and planning that went into a Double D Trailer, and we were particularly impressed with the safety features.

"We owned a European trailer in the past, and greatly appreciate the one-piece roof. Even sitting out in the 100-degree Carolina sun, the interior stays much more comfortable compared to our previous metal-roofed trailer.

"What impresses everyone the most? When we open the SafeTack© compartment! What a phenomenal feature.

"Our last trailer had a rear collapsible tack room. I had to build a rack to keep things off the floor and away from the horse urine. Space was cramped and difficult. The SafeTack© feature is easy to use, well balanced and has tons of space.

"We own a Bashkir Curly and a Paso Fino that we use for trail riding. We have had them in a front facing slant load for years. Both horses easily loaded into the rear facing position from both the side ramp and the rear ramp. Unloading the trailer was a breeze.

"Watching the horses travel on the integrated camera clearly shows they are calm the whole trip. They enjoy the oversized windows and exit without being overheated. Our Curly used to ride with his head down all the time. Now, he keeps his head up and likes to watch the world go by."

A well-insulated trailer can make all the difference for your horses, especially if you live or travel in hot temperatures. While you relax in your truck with your air conditioning on, your four-legged friends might be too hot back in the trailer. Quality, non-aluminum roof materials and adequate ventilation can make traveling much more enjoyable for your horses.

Say Goodbye to Loading Problems

When your horse likes your trailer, you'll know. There are many tell-tale signs your horse is enjoying their new ride — floppy, happy ears, a calm and relaxed semblance, and even eagerly chomping on hay during transit.

For many horses, loading into the trailer can be a hassle. If they've had a bad experience in the past or have been spooked by the trailer, they will be resistant and anxious during loading. But many times, the horse isn't the culprit — the trailer is!

Rachael K from Pennsylvania realized that was the case after struggling to load her horse time and time again. She says:

"My high-strung thoroughbred caused me major headaches for years because he wouldn't load onto the trailer. I remember many shows where we wasted hours in the morning trying to get him onto the trailer — even missing classes.

"One time we spent hours trying to get him to walk onto a friend's small, enclosed, two-horse trailer, but our ride had to leave without us.

"Then, just minutes after, we tried to walk him onto a different trailer with a much more open, airy design. He walked on within minutes! The type of trailer makes a huge difference."

Trisha from Ohio has a similar story. For years, her horses had no problems loading into the trailer. But suddenly, one of her horses became very nervous during loading time, and another became a very stubborn loader.

She said: "After years of having no problems, I found myself tearing out a rear tack because my horse refused to back out." She decided to go with a SafeTack© Reverse Load 2 Horse Gooseneck Trailer — and immediately saw what a difference it made.

"The day I received my trailer I took my problem loader to it. To my surprise the horse that usually puts up a 45-minute fight, self-loaded! And happily loads every time now."

The Right Trailer Can Prevent Dangerous Accidents

Trish was delighted her loading problems had disappeared, and she was also thrilled her new trailer kept her horses safe.

She said: "Last year one horse fell in the trailer. I was able to pull over, quickly get her out and reload. Only a small scratch on the knee. She could have easily slid under the other horse if the panel wasn't there."

Strong, durable, full-body dividers are essential for keeping your horses safe during travel. Just imagine what could have happened if Trish had a trailer with fragile dividers or ones with dangerous gaps. Her horse could have gotten stuck under the divider or even broken a leg.

A trailer needs to be much more than just shiny and beautiful to be the right one for you and your horses. While aesthetics are important, your horse's safety should always come first.

As you've learned throughout these pages, how the trailer is made — material choices, safety considerations, and design — makes a huge impact on the overall functionality and safety of your trailer.

Remember, buying a trailer is a luxury purchase, but always make sure you keep your horses in the forefront of your mind when deciding which trailer will be best for you. After all, your four-legged friends deserve a comfortable, enjoyable, and stress-free ride, too!

Brad's Trailer Tips & Takeaways:

- A horse trailer is a luxury that allows you to pursue your passion of horse riding, trail riding, equine events, and equine travel. Make sure you buy a trailer that's not just safe, but also one that meets all your expectations — this will ensure maximum satisfaction.

- Before you start shopping, define your needs clearly by asking three questions: How many horses do you need to haul? What trailer configuration is right for you? Can my tow vehicle haul my trailer?

- The true cost of a trailer is the difference in what you pay for it versus what you can sell it for.

- Research is key to making a good purchase. Make sure you research various trailer manufacturers, styles, and designs to find the trailer of your dreams — the one that's safe, beautiful, and aligned with a realistic budget.

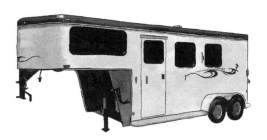

Recap of Key Points

The most important factors to consider when buying a horse trailer are you and your horse's safety and comfort, your priceline, and your wants as a horse owner. Remember, a horse trailer is a luxury purchase, and it should always meet — if not exceed — your expectations.

The key to a strong, durable, and solid trailer is using high-quality construction materials. Galvanized sheet metal, fiberglass roofs, steel/zinc composite frames, high-quality primer and paint, and Rumber flooring makes for a trailer that will stay beautiful and functional for years to come.

To know which trailer is best for you, decide how many horses you need to haul, whether you need living quarters or not, and what loading configuration your horses like. This will narrow down your choices of trailer designs and help you choose the one that's right for you.

The setup and design of your trailer can make loading your horses *much* easier. Side load options with wide doors, a welcoming, open, and clean entryway, customizable stalls, and ramps instead of step-ups all lead to a smoother loading and unloading process.

Choose a horse trailer manufacturer known for safety and quality. Don't be afraid to ask about the thickness and strength of the materials used to build the trailer, especially the trailer walls, frame, and dividers.

Your trailer is only as strong as the weakest link of the equation. That's why it's essential to have adequate tires and the correct suspension system, and make sure you can safely carry the load being hauled.

What a vehicle is capable of carrying is NOT the same as what it can tow. To haul your trailer safely, you must know the trailer's tongue weight and your tow vehicle's payload to assure your vehicle will carry it.

Get your trailer checked by a professional every year. Doing regular maintenance checks on your trailer, cleaning regularly, and keeping everything in proper condition is much less expensive than having to do costly trailer repairs.

When buying a trailer, set a realistic budget, but also remember that a horse trailer is a luxury and should meet all your requirements for maximum satisfaction, both for you and your horses.

Final Thoughts from Brad Heath

Some horse owners *dread* trailering their horses.

They think back to bad experiences they've had in the past where someone almost got hurt. Or they know their trailer is outdated, subpar, or on the verge of breaking down. Each trip becomes a game of Russian roulette — one that could go south very quickly.

But traveling with your horses should *always* be a comfortable, enjoyable, and fun experience.

After all, you're off to compete with your horses in equine competitions, trail ride through breathtaking scenery, and visit new, undiscovered places with your best four-legged friends. It's a grand adventure, and your horse trailer should make travel even better.

When you have the right trailer — one that's safe for you and your horses, reliable, and beautiful — traveling is *easy*. Having the right trailer will bring an enormous sense of confidence and ease. You'll know your horses are comfortable, you'll know your truck can handle the load, and you'll feel secure in your ability to get to the destination and back without any problems.

In this comprehensive guide, you've learned what safety features to look for, what designs and configurations work best, what materials are safest, and how to plan for safe towing. You should now have the knowledge and insights necessary to choose the *right* trailer — for you!

After 30 years of designing and building customized trailers for horse owners across the nation, I've realized this: **every horse owner needs a trailer that brings them the maximum value, safety, and joy.**

After all, isn't that why we own and love horses? They bring us happiness.

Your horse trailer is no different. Looking at it, driving it, traveling with it — heck, even cleaning it — should make you smile.

So, find one you truly love. One you're proud of. One that keeps you, your family, and your horses safe and protected. One that will take you to all your favorite places for years and years to come.

Yes, find a horse trailer that makes *you* happy.

About the Author

Brad Heath is the innovative force behind Double D Trailers, a custom horse trailer brand that has transformed the horse trailer industry over the last few decades. Drawing from his personal experience as a horse owner and his upbringing on a family farm, Brad is well equipped to share deep insights into the equestrian lifestyle.

Originating from a simple family-owned farm supply store started in 1994, Double D Trailers has evolved under Brad's leadership to become a premier name in horse trailer manufacturing. Brad's revolutionary designs, including the SafeTack© Reverse Slant Load Horse Trailer which garnered U.S. Patent #9132762, have set new standards in the industry.

He is renowned for his dedication to creating the safest trailers for both horses and handlers. This is evidenced by the unique features he has developed over the years, such as the SafeTack© compartment, which enhances the loading and unloading experience, and his emphasis on using materials that offer the right combination of safety, comfort, and durability.

Brad's entrepreneurial spirit extends beyond Double D Trailers. He is also the president of App Crafters, Inc., a company that aids entrepreneurs in finding tech solutions for online businesses.

Through his articles and appearances on various platforms, Brad has become a respected voice in the horse trailer safety domain, offering valuable insights to equestrians worldwide. His commitment to ensuring optimum safety for all is the cornerstone of Double D Trailers' ethos, making it a trusted name among horse enthusiasts.

Brad Heath's expertise, innovative approach, and unwavering dedication to the safety and well-being of horses and their owners have made him a distinguished figure in the equestrian community.

Connect with Brad Heath:
https://www.doubledtrailers.com
https://www.facebook.com/DoubleDHorseTrailers/
https://www.instagram.com/doubledtrailers/
https://dbradheath.com/

Glossary of Terms

air ride: electric- or engine-powered suspension that uses rubber air pumps rather than metal springs.

axle: a rod or shaft that connects and rotates the wheels while supporting the weight of your trailer.

billet: a semi-finished aluminum piece, around 8–10 inches in diameter, shaped like a long light pole; they are essential in the construction of aluminum horse trailers.

bumper pull: trailer configuration that uses a ball hitch attachment, connecting the trailer to the back of your tow vehicle; also known as tagalong trailers.

composite materials: a solid material made from two or more materials with different properties; for example, fiberglass, which is made of glass fibers, resin, and other materials.

dies: a device that serves as a mold that can impress or finish another object or material; these dies are used to shape aluminum billets during the construction process.

dividers: partitions between horses in a trailer, they should be strong, durable, and highly functional; most include head dividers and support the full length of your horse's body.

DOT: the U.S. Department of Transportation, they inspect both the exterior and interior of vehicles to ensure they are fit for travel and to increase safety on the road.

dressing room / tack room: a small closed-off area in the front of your trailer that can be used for storing equipment or changing into equine attire; this area is separate from the horse area, although some have a small door that leads into the horse area.

ELD (Electronic Logging Devices): a machine that synchronizes with your vehicle's engine to digitally record driving hours; required for some commercial drivers.

Galvanneal: galvanized sheet metal made for painting, this material does not rust and has superior strength and durability; this material is commonly used to make pickup truck beds.

GAWR (Gross Axle Weight Rating): the maximum amount of weight your trailer's axles can support.

gooseneck: trailer configuration for larger, heavier trailer models; these have a connector that hangs down from the front of the trailer and connects to a hitch mounted in the truck bed.

grommets: rubber or plastic materials that protect electrical wires from being damaged by vibration.

GVW (Gross Vehicle Weight): the weight of the trailer.

GVWR (Gross Vehicle Weight Rating): the maximum, fully loaded weight your trailer can support; this includes the weight of your trailer, the weight of your horses, and the weight of everything else (gear, hay, tack) in your trailer.

jack block: a metal or wooden block that goes under the jack for extra height, support, and stability.

leaf spring: commonly used type of suspension that has springs made up of strips of flat metal formed in an arc.

living quarters trailers: trailers specially designed for camping or overnighting; most have a kitchenette, small bedroom area, and living room space built into the front of the trailer.

mechanical fasteners: small metal pieces like rivets, screws, bolts, and washers that create a non-permanent bond between two materials.

payload: how much your vehicle can carry; to calculate this, subtract the weight of the vehicle from the GVWR.

rear saddle compartment: also known as a rear tack, this is a small storage closet either built in or attached to the rear loading area of the trailer — beware of built-in models, as they narrow the loading space.

reverse load: trailer design that allows your horses to face the rear of a horse trailer, rather than the front.

rubber torsion: also known as TORFLEX, this type of suspension works by twisting a thick piece of rubber inside a square tube.

Rumber: a horse trailer flooring material made from recycled tires; this material transfers the least amount of heat, noise, and vibration and is virtually indestructible.

SafeTack© compartment: a custom-built storage compartment proprietary to Double D Trailers; this storage space is mounted on hinges, allowing it to swing out like a second door, leaving a full-width entry way for easy loading and unloading.

sealant: material used for closing gaps during the construction process, making them airtight and watertight.

slam latch: type of locking configuration in which the horse trailer dividers slam into a latch to close and to open, the handler lifts the latch handle.

slant load: horse loading configuration in which the horses are at an angle in the trailer during travel; can be forward-facing or reverse-facing.

straight load: horse loading configuration in which the horses are parallel to the trailer walls during travel; can be forward-facing or reverse-facing.

strap hinge: a long, slim type of trailer hinge that folds almost 270 degrees (compared to the typical 180 degrees), allowing the door to fold around the sidewall of the trailer.

striker plate: the flat piece of metal with a hole that receives the spring-loaded latch to secure your door.

stud gates: a partition or divider that reaches all the way to the floor of the trailer and prevents kicking between horses.

tongue weight: how much your trailer weighs from the front end, where it connects to your truck. This is the amount of the load that's distributed to your tow vehicle during travel and not carried by the trailer's suspension.

uprights: vertical post-like rods or metal posts that form the structural support for a horse trailer.

VIN (Vehicle Identification Number): your trailer's serial number, stamped onto the vehicle by the manufacturer; this number is used during compliance checks.

walk-through: type of trailer design where a horse can load and unload without having to back up. In a rear-facing model, for example, the horse loads through a side door, walks into the stall, and exits through the back of the trailer.

3M VHB tape: a super-strong, tape-like waterproof chemical bonding technology that merges two pieces of metal together as one; this is one of the safest and most durable sealant options.

Frequently Asked Questions

Aren't steel trailers much heavier than aluminum trailers?

While steel does weigh more than aluminum, aluminum trailers use a lot more metal materials during construction in order to make them durable and safe. Usually, a well-built steel-frame trailer will weigh within 10% of a well-built aluminum trailer.

Will larger horses like warmbloods fit in a slant-load trailer?

Some slant-load trailers are designed to fit only smaller horses — usually up to 15.3 hand range. However, many trailer manufacturers like Double D Trailers can custom design slant-loads to fit any size horse.

Do horses haul better in a rear-facing configuration?

Research suggests that when hauled in a rear-facing position, horses experience less stress and are better able to balance. When left untethered in an open box stall trailer, the horse will almost always turn at a slant, facing away from the direction of travel.

What is the best type of material for horse trailer roofs?

Fiber composite stands out as the top choice for climate control and ease of maintenance in horse trailers. Fiber composite roofs are excellent for insulation and seamless, eliminating leaks and most maintenance needs.

Where do I find the total weight of my horse trailer?

The actual trailer weight is NOT shown on the VIN sticker or tire placard. To figure out how much your trailer weighs, you must weigh it at a truck scale weigh station.

What is weight distribution?

A weight distribution system is a special kind of hitch that allows you to haul the maximum capacity of your tow vehicle's hitch while improving towing safety. It is made up of a large trailer hitch, a weight distribution shank with a ball mount, and spring bars that mount under your horse trailer.

What pickup trucks are recommended for pulling a horse trailer?

Trucks that have towing limits greater than 7,000 lbs. are great options to pull horse trailers. Some pickup trucks recommended for pulling a horse trailer include: RAM trucks, Ford F150s, Toyota Tundras, and GMC Sierras.

Why does my horse refuse to load into my trailer?

Horses are naturally averse to dark, cramped spaces — if your trailer is uninviting, badly lit, and built with a narrow entry-way, it will be difficult to load a nervous horse. Some horses have had bad loading experiences in the past that scar them and create a fear of the trailer. To minimize loading difficulties, make sure your trailer is comfortable, well-lit, clean, and inviting, with a wide entryway.

How often should I clean my horse trailer?

Always do a quick clean after every trip, removing wet hay and other wet items that could cause mold. Remove mats and make sure you hose down any areas of the floor covered by urine. This is especially important if you have an aluminum floor as the urine can cause it to corrode and weaken over time. Monthly trailer cleaning will keep your trailer in top condition, and I recommend scheduling a deep cleaning every six months as well.

How do you remove rust on a horse trailer?

Wash, sand, prime, and paint the rusted area to remove rust. This will work for a couple of small rusted areas. However, if your trailer has multiple surfaces that are rusted-through, they should be professionally repaired. Rust can cause dangerous structural damage and should be taken seriously.

Where is the VIN on my horse trailer?

The VIN can usually be found on the trailer tongue or the front of the frame. If it's not there, it could be on the gooseneck, or the bottom part of the fender, or next to the fender. There are no regulations as to where the VIN needs to be, so it might take a little searching to find it.

How much does a horse trailer cost?

The price of a horse trailer depends on many factors: whether it's new or used, how many horses it can haul, the quality of the materials used, the manufacturer, and even the type of hitch. Used horse trailers can span anywhere from around $2,000 to well over $100,000, while new trailers can range from $10,000 up to $200,000 for some large, custom-built models.

How much does a bumper pull trailer typically cost?

A new bumper pull trailer typically costs anywhere from $10,000 to $40,000 or more.

What is a realistic price range for gooseneck trailers?

Average prices for gooseneck trailers range from $25,000 to $50,000 or more.

How much does a three-horse gooseneck trailer with living quarters cost?

Trailers with living quarters are typically the most expensive type of trailer, as they cost more to manufacture and are often highly customized. New trailers with living quarters can range anywhere from $30,000 to over $200,000. Used trailers can be a much more affordable option, although they might need more frequent repairs depending on the year they were made and the manufacturer.

Thank you for reading!

Learn more about Brad's trailer designs and grab your FREE GIFT at:

www.doubledtrailers.com/book

Made in the USA
Middletown, DE
12 July 2025